The soldiers took the Bibles out into the streets and burned them in one huge bonfire. Then the pastor was put in prison again. He had been in prison for nine years before that. He prayed, "Lord, You know the communists have taken every possible copy of Your Word. You have seen those copies burning. I ask You, would You please speak to someone *outside* of China? Would You cause them to prepare the Scriptures for our people?

"And Lord, would You bring those Bibles into our land?"

God's Smuggler to China

A CRY TO THE CHINESE TO LET US LOVE THEM

BROTHER DAVID

with Sara Bruce and Dan Wooding

LIVING BOOKS
Tyndale House Publishers, Inc.
Wheaton, Illinois

DEDICATION

To Julie, the 3 D's, and my mother
With all my love

Scripture quotations are from the King James
Version and the Revised Standard Version of the
Bible.

Library of Congress Catalog Card Number 81-50139
ISBN 0-8423-1083-5, Living Books Edition
Copyright © 1981 by Brother David and
Open Doors International with Brother Andrew.
All rights reserved.
First printing, February 1981.
Printed in the United States of America.

CONTENTS

FOREWORD
by Brother Andrew

It was fifteen years almost to the day that I was
again back on the Great Wall of China, to the
north of Peking. As I stood on this impressive for-
tification which winds snake-like for nearly 2,000
miles across the belly of the People's Republic, I
was reminded that it was originally built for a
special reason—to keep the barbarians out, the
Mongols who threatened the very lives of the
Chinese.

Since it was first built some 2,000 years ago, the
Chinese have built many more walls—political,
military, ideological, always designed to keep people with their beliefs out.

On the first occasion, I had stood amid the
crowds of unsmiling Chinese and claimed open
doors for China. I had asked in my prayer that the
Government of Mao Tse-tung could no longer be
able to keep people—God's people—out, with their
life-changing ideas.

Little did I know at the time that there was also
a man outside of China who was praying that
same prayer. That man was Brother David, an
extraordinary individual whose inspiring and
moving story you will read in this book. He was
saying, "God give us open doors to reach the
people. Give us people through whom You can
love China." God is a God who answers prayer,
as we have proved time and time again.

God's Smugglers to China will encourage you
to ask the biggest things of God and to expect the

biggest answers you've ever had through faith and prayer. Why? Because over these fifteen years God did open the doors to China, He did provide people to penetrate the Bamboo Curtain, and He gave a vision to a man very different from me, yet with the same burden, vision and faith.

In reading *God's Smuggler to China*, you will learn the exciting story of how God used my dear friend Brother David to make contact with the remaining believers in China; how He enabled him to find the churches there and to communicate with them; how God miraculously provided the contacts and the people so that they could trust them and us so as to make special requests for help.

Now they have asked and been supplied with thousands of Bibles. Many have replaced those destroyed in the Cultural Revolution, while others have been placed in the hands of those who have never owned a Bible. The ten million believers of China realize that there is no limit with God and have now asked for an initial one million Bibles. We have agreed to trust God for this number because we know those inside can use them as they work to reach all of China with the redeeming message of Jesus Christ.

As you read this book, you will see how God works, you will identify with Brother David and his brave team of people described in these pages. But more than that, you will see that God can do the same with *you*. He can use *you* to open up countries and continents and indeed the whole world for His message of love and salvation.

What God can do through one man, He can surely do through *you*.

ACKNOWLEDGEMENTS

This book tells more than my story. It is the story of God at work in and through a team of His people, including Brother Andrew and the church in China.

I am grateful to God for the encouragement Brother Andrew has been to me all these years, and for the tremendous team the Lord has placed around us and the suffering church in Asia. I am also grateful to God for all our friends in the United States who have supported and prayed for our ministry to the suffering church.

God's Smuggler to China is not a book I had planned to write. In fact, it very nearly didn't happen. Although Brother Andrew and Sven, our Open Doors international vice-president, consistently asked me for it, I was certain I could not meet their request.

I didn't. God Himself fulfilled that request. Psalm 57:2 says: "I cry to God most high, to God who fulfills his purpose for me" (RSV). The book has been *His* doing, since He has brought together a team to put it together.

The first to join the team was Marichelle Roque-Lutz, to whom I am very grateful for the six months of research and writing which she put into the first draft. After that, however, we had to wait twelve months before returning to the task. In the interim, God was very evidently at work in the ministry, and there was much more to tell.

Then, He brought an Australian family to the

Philippines to join hands with us and the suffering church. Sara Bruce shared with me the most in the writing, research, and development of this book. Through Sara's help, the team, Julie, and I were able to share the principles of the ministry and the witness of the Lord at work. Sara and I needed assistance, and so God brought a jolly Englishman, Dan Wooding, who spent many weeks working with us. From the depths of my heart I want to thank Sara Bruce and Dan Wooding. Without them, we wouldn't have a book.

Of course, the family from Australia were also to become back-up members of the team. While Sara was hard at work for long months, husband Michael and their two little boys gave her untiring care and support. Julie and I will long be indebted to them.

Other vital contributions to the book came from the Open Doors Asia staff members who gave time for interviews, research, and proofreading of the manuscript. My sincere thanks to them for taking time out of their already busy schedules.

My grateful thanks also to Shan Kumar for his editorial assistance, fellowship, and encouragement for the book as well as for the Asia ministry itself.

To Beng Tuazon, Lilith, Adel, Marcie, and the rest of the office staff who worked so hard on typing and xeroxing the manuscript, I give my sincere appreciation. Their corporate attitude can be summed up in the words of one young man who worked on the xerox machine for almost twenty-four hours straight, yet at the end could still say with a smile, "Thank you, Jesus!"

Behind-the-scene team members also included two very special Chinese families whose invaluable counsel helped shape the ministry to meet the needs of their people in China. Their fellowship, encouragement, and love, both for us and for

10

one another, have been in the true spirit of Jesus Christ. I am grateful to them for welcoming our team as members of their large Chinese family.

Likewise, my thanks to Bill Butler and his great team at Christian Resource Management for their guidance, support, and loving dedication.

The Lord brought all of these people into the ministry. Without them we wouldn't have had a story to tell.*

And, of course, particular thanks to the publishers for their helpful direction in the completion of the book.

Special gratitude to my very first "team members," Julie and our children who provided constant support and encouragement, even at a sacrifice to them. And with the book, Julie once again gave of herself during the long hours I worked to complete it.

In addition, Julie also took Sara Bruce across the border bridge at Lo Wu and introduced her to the People's Republic of China. Julie even participated in the research and carefully proofread the manuscript. Above all, I am grateful for her most vital role: praying for the completion of the book, often far into the night.

Finally, my heartfelt thanks and praise to the Lord Himself for bringing the necessary people, tools, and resources. The book has been His doing, not mine!

He is truly fulfilling His purposes for us and our Chinese friends. The work is going on.

Brother David

---

*Their names, as with almost all those in the book, have been changed to protect their ministry to the suffering church. Locations and names of believers inside China have also been changed for their own protection.

A Note to the Reader

In this book, we have adopted the Pinyin system of romanizing Chinese names. Since January 1, 1980, the Pinyin system has been in official use in all documents published in the People's Republic of China. The system was developed by the Chinese themselves; "Pinyin" means "spelling the sound."

The older systems, such as Wade-Giles and Yale, while more familiar to the Western eye, have now been more or less discarded by newspapers, journals, et cetera, dealing with China. These publications have followed the Chinese changeover.

For the reader's benefit, we have placed the older, perhaps more familiar spelling in parentheses, next to the new spelling at its first appearance.

ONE

AGAINST NEW ODDS

"These people have sinned against the State." The officer's angry voice rang out over the large crowd. "Now they will pay the price—the ultimate price."

As guards released the safety catches on their rifles, Mrs. Kwang prayed, "Father, forgive them. They know not what they do."

"Take aim. Fire!" The crack of rifle shots echoed through the square as bullets flew into the men and women lined up before them. Many instantly slumped to the ground, while others remained standing. Among those unhurt was Mrs. Kwang.

"If you engage in counter-revolutionary activity, you will face the same death," the communist leader warned the crowd. Then, turning on his heel, he marched his men from the square.

Mrs. Kwang and the other survivors walked slowly back to join the hushed onlookers. After this incident, many believers became fearful, and many lost their faith. The church in China had begun to discover who the real believers were. A purifying fire would reveal it all.

This account of Mrs. Kwang was one among many which her son, Daniel Kwang, shared with me during the preparation for one of our largest Bible delivery projects: Project Rainbow. We were planning to send 30,000 Scriptures at one time into China.

The whole venture boggled my mind. But the

Lord had already brought me and my family through some difficult times—just as He had with Mrs. Kwang. Hadn't I learned enough by now to trust Him? Hadn't I come through a few of my own battles?

"You're a bunch of babies. You don't know how to make a bed properly. You do not understand yet that in the U.S. Marine Corps men make beds that will put chambermaids of the Hilton Hotel to shame." Sergeant Hall's voice boomed out.

Outside our barracks, sixty-five of us in Platoon 150 stood at stiff attention.

Sergeant Peters, another drill instructor, handed him a cup of coffee. Sipping the coffee, Sergeant Hall began pacing up and down our ranks. Occasionally he scrutinized several among us carefully. He snickered openly as if recalling a private joke.

Then he stood in front of me. I pulled my stomach in and held my breath. He made a big production of slowly inspecting me from head to toe.

Suddenly, without warning, he threw the cup of steaming coffee straight at my chest. I flinched, stepping back in reflex, as the hot coffee seeped through my fatigue uniform. The tips of my ears tingled as adrenalin shot into my bloodstream. *No, Dave!* I commanded myself. I gritted my teeth and forced my anger down, the picture of my calm, disciplined father coming to mind. When he saw my reaction, his smirk changed into an amused grin.

"Clown, why don't you pick up that cup?" He pointed to the now empty cup on the ground.

"I'm at attention," I answered. He stiffened.

"I'm at attention, WHO?" His voice hissed for a strike.

"Sir, I'm at attention," I said, correcting my mistake.

14

"Why didn't you catch my cup of coffee, Butterball?" I racked my brain for the right answer. Dared I answer at all?

"Sir, because I'm sloppy, Sir." The answer pleased him.

"You're g—d— right you're sloppy. All dumbbells are." He sauntered away. He was through with me.

But he was not through with us. Back and forth he went, in his lazy, arrogant stance. And then, the smirk continuously playing about his lips, he delivered his parting speech.

"I like you boys. You have the nerve to appear before the U.S. Marine Corps command looking like a bunch of girls and believing, actually believing, that the U.S. Marine Corps can make men out of you! Such gall. Well, you're g—d— right we're going to change you into men, if it kills you. This is the Marine Corps of the United States. We make men. We break clowns, sissies, and slobs. That just about covers all of you here.

"Boy, you're the sorriest-looking batch I've ever encountered in all my years in San Diego. Nerve, that's what you've got. . . ."

Suddenly the Sergeant stopped acting. His impressive baritone rang out: "Well, d____it. You want to change into Marines. We *will* change you into Marines. It won't be easy. Not on your part, not on ours. Many of you will be squealing 'wee, wee' all the way to your mothers. But for those among you who can survive thirteen weeks of hell in bootcamp, you will have the singular honor, the prestige, of being called—no, of *being*—a U.S. Marine!"

Sergeant Hall was not exaggerating. The initial weeks of obstacle courses were just the beginning of a physical, mental, and emotional nightmare intended to build or break a man's body and spirit. We were insulted, physically and mentally assaulted, and driven past the breaking point.

I was determined not to give in. I was committed to turning myself into a good Marine—a successful Marine. Ever since childhood I'd known failure. At ten years of age, I could neither read nor write. I desperately wanted to and tried hard to overcome a reading handicap but couldn't. I felt defeated since I was two grades behind kids my own age.

"David, Group Four, the beginner books," my third-grade teacher always said. Slowly the message began to sink in: "You're a second-rate student. You won't ever be any good in school."

My parents tried to help me. "You can do it, David," my dad often said. "Keep trying." Finally, after a lot of moving around the country and my attending a lot of different schools, my family settled in one place where the school took a real interest in helping me. My problem was later diagnosed as *severe* dyslexia. It wasn't a problem of thinking, but of inaccurate perception.

In time, my grades improved, but reading remained a struggle for me, even through high school.

In ninth grade I found that football was my arena for achievement. Out on the field I had to knock heads with older guys who seemed twice as big as I, but nothing could keep me from the pleasure of the game.

After one very strenuous game, my coach came up to me and said how proud he was of me. "Say, did you know the scouts were here for the game?" he asked me. "After tonight, they'll be watching for you. If you keep up that standard of playing, you might find yourself walking into the arms of one of the best universities in the country."

His comment seemed unbelievable to me at the

time, considering my poor academic record. Yet, when graduation came, I was one of the two awarded a football scholarship.

At the University of Denver, I did well on the football gridiron, but struggled in the student's chair. My reading slowness still plagued me, and logarithms were dragging down my math grade. In short, I realized that after eighteen months at the university, the academic battle was not going to get any easier. So I took a "semester off," but never returned.

My parents were patient, and encouraged me to find a job. They told me about a vacancy in a lithography shop downtown. "Would you be interested?" my Dad asked, without pressuring me.

I applied for the job and got it. I began right away enjoying the new challenge. Soon, I started fitting in with my buddies at work. Joining them for booze, gambling, and girls, I had a new image. I wasn't a kid anymore.

The only place I didn't feel quite comfortable was home—there I lived a double life. Somehow, as I looked into my father's face and saw the integrity etched in every line, I couldn't let him know about my "extra-curricular" activities. I felt the same about my mother, who had determined we live life as "God meant us to live it."

To please them, I complied with their request that I attend church with them week after week. Then, something happened which made me resolve never to attend a church meeting again. I'd planned on seeing Jayne Mansfield, the famous movie star, get married in a nearby town. I was counting off the days until I could see her with my own eyes.

"The church has a special meeting, son, and I think you ought to be there," my father told me on the day of the Mansfield wedding.

"But, Dad, tonight's the night when. . . ."

"David, I'm not *asking* you to go. I'm *telling* you!"

I went. And the evening turned out to be a complete disaster. The meeting at church was a fund-raising session for a new building drive. The organizers said they knew my income must be over five thousand dollars, so they were counting on me to help with financial support.

"We've come up with a figure we think you could comfortably afford each month. How about it?"

That did it! By the time I got home, I was seething with fury. To think that I had missed seeing Jayne Mansfield for that church meeting.

"Dad? Mom? You listen, and listen good! I've had it with that church of yours. Up to here. As far as I'm concerned, you can take your church and go to hell!"

I knew I had gone too far, so I wasn't surprised when my mother disciplined me with a leather strap. But one thing wouldn't change: Wild horses couldn't drag me back inside a church again.

Before long, Uncle Sam tapped on my shoulder, and I decided to enlist in the Marines. I wanted to be the best Marine I could be!

After the early weeks of training, the "sissies" in our platoon began to look more like Marines. The thin ones filled out with solid muscles; the fat ones melted down. After some months, nobody recognized us. Our bodies had hardened into bullets. Just like our minds, spirits, and characters. The Marine Corps had one goal: To change us into men willing to kill and to die in defense of our country.

Once when I lifted my hands, I realized how strong they'd become during training. *Thanks to that, I now have a killer's instincts,* I thought proudly.

Immediately, I knew I had lied. Paradoxically, in mastering the art of killing, I had lost all desire to fight.

Why had I joined the Marines? For love of country. To belong to America's finest class of men. For love of action and a challenge. To fulfill my childhood dream. To prove a point. Any of these reasons or all of them combined. But was I really satisfied?

At the end of my service, I left to resume work as a lithographer. My parents welcomed their ex-Marine son with open arms.

It took me no time at all to settle down in my old job. I liked the work and even more, the company of my buddies who worked there. Every day, after work, we went to a club in Gardenia, the only town in California where gambling was legalized. Food and drink were cheap there to lure people into the gambling.

In the cocktail lounge, we downed one drink after another. I always made sure I drank just as much as the others. After all, I had an image to project. And every part of it had to be just right.

We'd swap stories of our "chicks," each boast gaining in the telling. My versions were often sprinkled with the salty language I'd picked up in the Marines.

But if I were really honest with myself, I'd have to admit I'd never liked drinking, even from the beginning. I'd seen the dignity stripped from any-one who had drunk himself stupid. Still I went right into it. I'd had enough of being different from everyone. Now I had the chance to show the world I wasn't second-rate any more.

I tried reassuring myself that what I was into was right. Somehow even that wasn't enough, though. The louder my jokes and boasts, the more hollow they sounded in my own ears.

Meanwhile, drinking helped lull me into a state of oblivion. I had girls, liquor, and friends. Most of all, I was accepted. But deep down, was I really happy?

Then I met Julie Porter. After two weeks, we were both smitten with each other. I never let a single day go by without seeing her. We laughed together, went driving and sightseeing together, and ran on the beach.

Every weeknight I had to travel across town for special classes to improve my reading and writing skills. Then, right afterwards I'd be at Julie's house at 10:00 P.M. sharp. We'd have Coke and potato chips. I'd tell her about my reading problem, and she'd patiently listen and gently encourage me with the homework. I, in turn, listened as she unburdened her problems of the day.

We had only one area of difference. Like my parents, Julie was serious about her religion. She'd made a commitment to Jesus Christ twelve months before. But she never talked about my beliefs. She said very little, in fact, about her own. It was her life that spoke volumes.

One evening I watched her taking care of her invalid eighty-year-old grandmother. I saw how carefully she fed her, washed her face and hands, cleaned her room, and fluffed up her pillows. Then, she sat beside the old woman to hear her reminisce.

This girl knew what it meant to care.

After meeting Julie, I couldn't be bothered with the other girls anymore. She had a depth which was new to me. She stood for something—and whatever it was, it rang true. It seemed that the girls I had known previously were mere carbon-copies compared to her. Julie was real, and I was head-over-heels in love.

After six months, our talks included new topics. The two of us started discussing our wedding, our marriage, the life we would share together. We planned on three children, each of them twenty months apart. We even chose their names.

Soon after, we got engaged. Then, after two months, we decided to elope, instead of waiting for the formal wedding my parents had hoped for.

Heading south, we crossed the border to Mexico. No one knew, except my boss at work, and two friends who came along as witnesses. To us, all that mattered was hearing the magic words: "I now pronounce you husband and wife." I kissed Julie and led her proudly from the tiny wedding chapel.

"What have you been doing in Mexico?" the American immigrations officer asked as we headed across the border on the way back.

"Eloping," I smiled. "Look, here's my wife's ring."

"How old is your wife?" he asked, leaning into the car and fixing his eye on Julie.

"She's eighteen," I replied.

"Young man, you ought to be ashamed of yourself."

I smiled. I wasn't ashamed. It was a border crossing I would never forget.

TWO
FIRST STEPS

I loved loving Julie. If, beforehand, I had expected marriage with her to be good, now that it had come about, I realized it was the best thing that had ever happened to me.

In time, as planned, we had our three babies, twenty months apart, and under Julie's gentle care, each of them healthy and gorgeous. We gave them the names we had chosen so long before: Deanne, Dawn, and David—our three "D's."

But as they grew, Julie became concerned about one aspect of their upbringing which was missing.

"Dave, the children really need to go to Sunday school."

"Honey, you know how I feel about church," I told her.

It was the first time the difference in our beliefs had disturbed the placid sea of our marriage.

For many years I had kept my resolution never to worship again. Since meeting Julie, I had attended a few times, but only for her sake. In church I always felt like a fish out of water. I didn't belong with the holy Joes gathered in those buildings. All of them always tried to save me— from what I wasn't sure. I only knew I'd be much happier if they just tried to get to *know* me instead.

On the weekends, I preferred the gambling tables to the local church bench. Julie's patience was incredible. She never nagged me into changing my ways, nor into allowing her to go to church.

The kids started Sunday school and our life went on as before. I was more than content with the way it was going. We were happy. I was doing well at the job. With plenty of overtime work, our bank balance was healthy. Life was everything I wanted.

Then, two of my drinking and gambling buddies got killed in two separate accidents. "Jesus!" I called out when I read about the second accident in the morning papers. "Jesus!" It was the first time I had ever called that name with any real meaning. Julie found me a trembling bundle of tears. She put her arms around me, thinking my tears were for my dead friends. I knew better. I was crying and shaking for myself.

Julie and my parents had been encouraging me to attend a Billy Graham Crusade which was soon coming to our area. I flatly refused. But after two weeks of their persistent requests, I gave in and said I'd go. The date was September 4, 1963.

That evening turned my life around. Billy Graham's message pierced through my tough Marine veneer. He quoted John 4:24: "God is spirit, and those who worship him must worship in spirit and truth."

Truth. What did I know about truth? Those aggravating doubts surfaced again. *You're not living the truth, David. You're out there proving yourself to everybody: the success story, the self-made man earning his way in the world with the things that matter. But are they the things that matter? You can't even explain death within your definition of life.*

What's got into me? I wondered. *These aren't the thoughts of a U.S. Marine. They must be due to the six cans of beer I drank before I left home.* But despite my attempts to explain it away, the questioning persisted.

Even the booze, David, the bars, the gambling,

the stories you always have up your sleeve, they are not giving you what you want, are they? For the first time I was ready to admit the truth. I had sold out to a lie and been conned by it.

The preacher continued. "You know, if you want to meet Jesus Christ, you've got to be prepared to let Him deal with sin in your life. He wants to save you from all that."

Okay, I thought, *if sin is the same as the lie I have been living, I've had enough of it anyway.*

"And," continued Billy Graham in his flowing Southern accent, "you have to let Jesus become the boss of your life, the Lord of your life."

I saw people stepping out from their seats and going to the front of the platform. If I did the same, it would mean that once again I'd have to be different and risk losing the friends I felt accepted by. But I'd also be throwing off the counterfeit for the true.

"I assure you that unless you change and become like little children, you'll never enter the kingdom of heaven. The Bible says this in Matthew chapter 18, verse 3. There is someone here tonight in his late twenties God is speaking to. He's telling that person to humble himself like a little child. A little child doesn't have to understand it all, yet he believes. . . ." I felt he was speaking to *me.*

"Now when you stand up and take the first step, Jesus will meet you and walk with you down here—and for the rest of your life. . . ." I stood up and tentatively edged my way to the aisle. When I reached the first step going down, an extraordinary thing happened. It was as though Someone had met me. I couldn't explain it, but when I got to the front, I recognized this Someone as Jesus, the One to whom Billy Graham was calling me to commit myself.

After prayer and some talk with a white-haired

Christian man named Mr. Roy, I turned to walk back to Julie. I knew that my life, too, was turning—never to be the same again. That same Presence Who had accompanied me all the way to the front stayed with me as I climbed those 120 steps back to my wife.

He has never left me since.

My lifestyle changed. People at work noticed a new person in me. Drinking stopped being a problem. I knew it had nothing to do with my own willpower or self-discipline. It was as though Jesus had literally lifted the old interests from me. And I loved Him for it.

The crap tables and the centerfolds which had papered the walls of my office no longer captivated me. The lifestyle I'd enjoyed before now seemed unattractive. It had all the appeal of a week-old loaf of bread. For the first time I felt really free!

Jesus had become the most important factor in my life. But the church hadn't.

"You need fellowship, David," old Mr. Roy insisted. "You need the support of others and also the teaching."

Inwardly, I battled, knowing that the lives of some who claimed to be Christians didn't match up with their words. They were a bunch of hypocrites. And the unforgettable night of missing Jayne Mansfield's wedding was still in my mind.

"David, I know the church is made up of human beings, and they make mistakes," Mr. Roy told me. "But you're a human being too, and so am I. Why do you think Jesus died for us? There's a way you can get your eyes off human failing and back on the One you're there for."

"What's that?"

"Service, son. Find a way to serve the others."

Eventually we started attending church regularly and began playing an active role in it. We even began tithing, although reluctantly since my overtime work had stopped and our budget had become tight. Amazingly, though, within a few days I was again asked to work overtime. Our income then increased to the point where we had more than enough for our needs!

As the weeks passed into months, we were happier than we had ever been before, except for one thing. A feeling of unrest had begun growing inside me. I had a feeling that while I was busy in my lithography job, I should actually be working somewhere else.

I even wrote the Billy Graham Association and shared with them my feelings of being unsettled. Their reply came quickly: "Wait patiently on the Lord, David. Meanwhile, concentrate on four areas: prayer, Bible reading, fellowship, and witnessing."

I'd already been involved in the first three areas, so following their advice, I got involved in an outreach program teaching football to some black young people. We also shared the gospel with them and soon had a group of twenty new believers, sweaty from work-out, meeting for fellowship. While we really got to know and love these youngsters, I still felt restless.

One day while reading Psalm 68, I was struck by verse 11: "The Lord gave the word: great was the company of those that published it." The word *published* stood out, as if in capital letters. Just one week earlier, I'd run across Mark 13:10: "And the gospel must first be published among all nations." *Published*! The word tied in with my line of work.

Was it possible that the Lord was directing me through verses?

"Honey, you don't suppose the Lord might call us to some place in the world where Bibles need to be printed?" I asked Julie right away. She suggested I ask our pastor, Kelly Walberg, who had a heavy burden for missions.

Pastor Walberg suggested we attend a meeting featuring someone from the Far East Broadcasting Company. I'd already heard excellent reports about their work of beaming gospel broadcasts throughout Southeast Asia, especially communist or restricted countries. China was the main country they were focusing on.

The representative we heard described the ministry. They needed an assistant in literature to help with the printing of Bibles for distribution among the countries of their region.

I don't have what it takes to be a missionary, I thought. Yet in time, I couldn't deny the facts. We'd asked God for a definite leading, and it seemed He was clearly pointing us in this direction. I came to believe we were to apply for that literature position available in Manila.

Our deacons at church evidently had the same conviction. Without our knowledge, they had approved a resolution supporting me and Julie for the first term of our literature ministry with FEBC!

We went ahead and applied for the position. Now we were waiting for the reply.

"Honey," Julie sobbed on the phone one day when I was at work. "They don't want us. . . . I'm so sorry. . . ."

We'd been so sure this was the right move for us. How could the answer be *no*?

The next day, FEBC phoned Julie, and she in turn phoned me at work. "They said for us to disregard the letter saying they can't use us. We're being recommended as missionary candidates after all!" The excitement in Julie's voice was contagious.

The Lord had broken through! Now we really knew we were following His direction.

Two weeks later I found out what had changed their minds. When I asked a representative from FEBC, he told me, "Didn't you know your church board members had committed themselves to you? We got their letter after we'd already written you back. By then, we realized the Lord was telling us *we'd* made a mistake."

THREE
BREAKING NEW GROUND

The following months flew by as we organized our household for the coming move. It was hard to leave our friends: Pastor Walberg, old Mr. Roy, the black kids, the teenagers in a group Julie and I had started, other couples at church, my buddies at work. Hardest of all was the wrench from our families, as we stepped out into an unknown future.

During our final days of packing, however, we had an unforgettable reminder of the One Who would be going with us. It happened the night when I was preparing our household goods for shipment to Manila. Our belongings had been transported to a large warehouse, and I had stayed behind to build a wooden crate around them. At midnight I returned home for some sleep, but was soon back at the warehouse to complete the job.

At six A.M. I finally left the building, only to discover my keys missing. I found a large hole in my pocket, through which the keys had no doubt fallen. But where?

Starting at one end of the building, I retraced my steps slowly for a full hour. I searched on hands and knees, without success. Then, I had a sudden conviction that the Lord was telling me, "Son, you're in the right position, but you're doing the wrong thing."

Of course, I realized I was on my knees. His voice seemed to continue: *I could have told you all along where they are. But you didn't ask Me.*

"Dear Father, forgive me," I said. "I never even

thought to pray about those wretched keys." It suddenly seemed so clear. Why had I come so far in my search without consulting Him? "But Father, I do ask You now, in Jesus' strong Name."

When I opened my eyes, I saw the shining gleam of metal only four feet away. "Thank you, Father," I almost shouted, running to the car.

A few minutes later, I reached the church property. Absentmindedly, I put my keys back into the pocket with the hole. A loud clink made me realize I had lost the keys again, this time in a hedge.

Groaning at my carelessness, I began a second hunt for them. The foliage was very dense. I thought I'd lost them for sure. Dropping to the ground, I crouched on my knees. Then, just as the first time, I sensed the Lord's voice again. *"Son, haven't you learned your lesson yet?"*

I hadn't. I was down on my knees again—in the right position, but doing the wrong thing. "Dear God, I'm sorry. Don't lose patience with me yet! Please, where are they *now*?" Opening my eyes, I reached into the bushes and placed my hands right on the keys.

The lesson seemed too incredible for words. And yet, maybe it wasn't. Perhaps the Lord was reassuring me in the most unmistakable way that He could take care of me and my family right down to the smallest detail.

When we finally reached the Philippines, the Lord had another surprise for us. Hanging outside our house in the FEBC compound was a huge sign welcoming every member of our family. Later, a specially prepared book was presented to us. In it were photographs of all the families on the compound with captions describing the roles of the parents, as well as the ages and interests of their children. The book was ours to keep.

Our final goodbye to our friends and family in

the States had been a tearful one. We knew it would be some years before we would see any of them again. But Jesus had proved faithful again. We knew we had family in Manila—God's family. We knew there would be no chance of loneliness there.

There were more lessons to learn during our early days with the broadcasting company. Although I knew that the Lord had brought us to FEBC, I felt inadequate to fulfill the role of missionary. Still young in Him, I wondered how I could minister to others.

Before long, it became obvious that God had that in hand, too. He was training me on the job, and each lesson was going to be painful.

Item number one on His list must have been the task of making me face myself honestly to clarify my values. My first morning on the job, I was enthusiasm itself.

A nearby press was churning out thousands of copies of the Gospel of John, all requiring someone to staple them together by hand. Was this to be my laborious job for the next few days, weeks, who knew how long? Was this why I'd been called to the mission field? Surely not.

But *yes*. All I'd be doing is stapling. Hour after hour that day, I sweated under the heavy weight of the debilitating humidity and the humility of the job. So it went until the long days turned into equally long weeks. Why had I trained all these years as a lithographer? It took no skill and no brains at all to do this work—nothing but time. In the States I'd held a far more responsible position. There, my daily routine had included clinching deals to bring in thousands of dollars for the business.

Each day the contrast loomed before me. Then, the Lord gave me some sledge-hammer thoughts:

David, what do you want? To go out and get rich? Or to follow Me? That morning I saw my work through new eyes. It was slow work and neither I nor the organization was making much money. But the Gospels we were producing were tools to change people's lives.

In the months that followed, I began to see the full breadth of FEBC's ministry. Its twenty-three broadcasting stations beamed daily programs inside the Philippines to other countries in Southeast Asia.

After "apprenticing" with the stapling machine, I began installing new equipment and later assisted in production management. Julie was busy editing tapes, part time, for the radio section of the ministry.

We had little spare time. But what little I did have, I channeled into another ministry to young people. With Robert Foster, also from FEBC, I worked among the teenagers on the streets of downtown Manila.

Twelve months after our arrival in the Philippines, we'd begun to feel very settled at FEBC. Then, a call from home jolted us. My father had died suddenly.

Almost as though reading my thoughts, my mother said, "I'm sure you're thinking you should come home. Well, don't. Your father would have wanted you there, where God means you to be. He would have wanted you to go on serving Jesus."

Julie and I felt strangely bereft. We couldn't accept the fact that Dad, the calm, thoughtful soul whom nothing could ruffle, would no longer be around to talk through problems. He wouldn't see his grandchildren grow up. Mother's house would be strangely silent without him and the steady stream of young people who always came to our home, seeking his wise counsel.

We battled our grief through the remainder of the morning. Then an understanding friend came by and prayed with us. In the quiet of that moment I comprehended more clearly than ever before, that to be absent from the body was to be present with the Lord.

I was at peace when I finally left the house and walked slowly back to work.

The literature production began to expand as FEBC took on contract work for other organizations. We were producing thousands of tracts for different groups, as well as distributing Gospels of John throughout the entire Philippines. After sending out a million Gospels, however, our team began re-evaluating the work. These islands were getting masses of gospel literature, but there were other countries getting hardly any at all. Wasn't it time we investigated their need for Scriptures as well?

For me, this was the start of frequent trips to assess the situation in some of our neighboring countries. Indochina was the main one on the list. In time, a second million Gospels of John were produced for that land.

Wartorn Vietnam was a particular focus for my travels. I regularly visited missionaries who had chosen to stay there during the Tet Offensive. Surrounded by troops, gunfire, and shelling, these brave men and women were determined to remain as long as possible, even though some of their colleagues had already been killed.

In time, the trips brought orders from many groups: Wycliffe Bible Translators, The American Bible Society, Christian and Missionary Alliance, the Southern Baptists, and many more. At the same time we had maintained our regular production for literature needed in the Philippines.

Each of these experiences provided training for me in a different kind of school. My "Teacher" still had a great deal to show me about the meaning of trusting Him in situations beyond my ability to cope.

One of those involved the care of my family. For me, security had always been tightly bound up with the mighty dollar. At FEBC, there were periods when our financial support would be held up due to various obstacles, particularly the erratic nature of the postal system. At one stretch, it was sixty days between checks; for the entire period, we had only forty dollars to our name.

During that time, there were evenings when the five of us would sit down at the supper table and thank God for empty plates. After praying, we'd spend the meal hour just enjoying one another's company. Later, we'd go to bed, committing ourselves once again into the Lord's care and trusting Him for the following day.

The Lord never allowed our hunger to last long. Although our principle was to tell no one but *Him* of our need, somehow bundles of food would "arrive" in our kitchen just at the right time. Sometimes after having gone out for a family walk around the compound, we would return to find that some other FEBC family had left a sack of provisions inside our back door. We'd find eggs, meat, canned food, vegetables, fruit—all the basics. To this day, we've never learned which families put them there.

One morning while Julie was preparing our daughter Deanne for school, there was no food for lunch. "Father, I want to trust you," Julie whispered quietly, "and I know we are here in Your will. You won't allow any need to go unmet." Then, she reached into the cupboard for a paper bag in which to place the nonexistent lunch. At that moment there was a tap on the window.

"Can I come in for a minute?" It was Leila, one of our neighbors. "I've made one too many sandwiches this morning. Would Deanne like an extra one?"

At other times, Julie would have the basic lunch ready, when again a knock would come, this time with an extra cookie or cake to brighten up lunch. It was just that additional touch from the Lord showing He cared even about the little things.

One steamy Sunday afternoon Julie and the children were sleeping through the siesta hour. The air hung still and thick with the crushing humidity of the tropics. Downstairs, in the kitchen, I was trying to cool myself with ice water in one hand and a fan in the other.

"Excuse me, sir," a little girl's voice broke the oppressive silence. "Please, I need help."

I opened the door cautiously. "Help" usually meant money. And we had almost none left. "Hello. What can I do for you?" I asked.

She looked embarrassed. "My father is waiting at the gate. Would you be the one to help him, sir?"

I followed the poorly clad girl to the entrance. There a frail-looking man greeted me. Gaping sores covered his legs.

"You are very kind to come, sir. I need help."

"What for?" I asked.

"I have leprosy, sir. I have been told of a place where I can go to be cured. But I do not have the bus fare." It was obviously an effort for him to ask for money, and he looked at the dust in shame.

"What is your occupation?" I said, stalling for time in an effort to avoid giving any of our depleted funds away. Why us, of all people, and at that particular time?

"I'm a pastor," he replied. "I hope to come back to my church when I'm cured."

"How much do you need?"

"Twenty pesos, sir."

Twenty pesos! At that time, the exchange rate was four pesos to one U.S. dollar. He was asking for exactly five dollars—all the money we had left.

"Surely not, Lord," I protested silently. "Do You really mean me to give it all away?" Even before I'd finished the prayer, I knew the answer.

"I have twenty pesos with me," I told the man as I reached reluctantly into my back pocket. "Here, take it. God bless you." I meant it; at least, I tried hard to.

After praying with them, I turned and slowly walked back to our home.

Once back in the kitchen, I laid it all before the Lord. "Father, I've done my best to obey You. You have led us out here, and we believe we have been following You. We left everything we had built up in America, and now we have nothing left here either. You've asked for everything and we've given it."

Then it was too much for me. I bowed my ex-Marine head and cried, my whole body shaking with emotion. How could I tell my wife that now we had nothing? And how could the children be expected to understand?

Even as I wept, a sense of reassurance came over me. My tears subsided. I told the Lord that I trusted and loved Him. I knew He was taking care of us, no matter what.

The following day, a letter arrived from Redondo Beach, California. Inside was a check for us. Our home church had sent $1,000!

FOUR
CLEARER VISION

"Why did You give us that press? Satan is laughing to see it lying there idle," I asked the Lord.

Nearly every machine at FEBC was faithfully churning out reams of Christian material; that is, all but one. The largest of them all, a Fairchild ColorKing press, stood useless in the corner. Donated by an American businessman, it could produce 20,000 Gospels of John in a single hour. It didn't make sense for God to lead someone to give such a gift and then have it sit idle.

A few weeks later, part of the answer to my question came in a hard-to-recognize form. Julie had persuaded me to take some time off to relax with the family at a local swimming pool. An afternoon of lazing around suited me fine. And the cool water proved to be a refreshing tonic.

"Hello," a roguish voice called out. It was Peter Jones, a friend with a ministry among the Chinese.

What do friends talk about while floating in a pool on a warm, tropical April day? Everything light and carefree, surely. I don't know why Jones and I had to discuss our work, but he couldn't keep from talking about his work, while I couldn't get off the topic of literature.

"Are you prepared to get Scriptures into China if it opens up?"

Is he serious? I thought. Why had he popped an improbable question like that? Everyone knew that Mao Zedong (Mao Tse-tung) had locked the country tighter than a drum. Even at that moment, the Great Helmsman was ruthlessly trying to eradicate all traces of pre-communist economy, religion, and culture in order to establish Marxist ideals.

Mao's Cultural Revolution, begun in 1966 and led by the teenage "Red Guards," had left in its wake three years of unparalleled chaos and suffering. Thousands were in prisons or re-education camps and thousands more were dead.

"You've got to be crazy," I told Jones. "China's never going to open up. Anyway, we're busy with Vietnam right now."

"David, don't say 'never.' Czechoslovakia was once considered closed to the world. But it opened up for a short time. When that happened, what did the missionaries do about it? Do you know?"

I didn't know. I'd never really thought about it. It was only much later that I learned that on the very day the Soviet tanks were rumbling into Prague to crush the liberal regime of Aleksander Dubcek, a slender Dutchman had also entered the city. Loading up his station wagon with tracts and Bibles, he had deliberately driven in among the massive tanks. He was determined to make the most of the last opportunity to distribute the Word of God freely among the Russian and Czechoslovakian people. His name was Brother Andrew.

Peter was insistent. "You see, David, *we* have to be *prepared*. If, someday, China does open up again, will you be ready?"

I already knew the answer. Of course I wasn't. To my knowledge, nobody was. The last of the missionaries had fled China by the early fifties. I hadn't met one who believed China would open up again. It seemed too incredible.

But the question kept going around in my head. Until then, I'd believed radio was the only way to get the gospel beyond the Bamboo Curtain. And yet, I also knew the promise in Psalms that with God's help, a person could leap over walls. God was going to have to teach me a great deal before I could really apply that promise to the impenetrable country of China.

One evening in May 1969 found me and an FEBC colleague kneeling together in prayer.

We had two questions for God: Was China going to open up? And if so, should we already be getting Scriptures prepared?

I agonized on my knees as we prayed, "Lord, please speak to us through Your Word, and please, would You tell us within the next fifteen days? If You don't let us know in that time, we will completely forget the whole crazy idea."

A few days later, I woke up at 2:30 A.M., strangely disturbed. At first, I tried to go back to sleep, but I sensed I was being prompted to stay awake. More than that, something, or Someone, appeared to be telling me to go down to the printshop.

I'd begun to recognize the still small voice of the Lord instructing me to do things; this time I felt sure I was hearing it once again. But the last thing I wanted was to visit my work place at that hour. Protest as I might, the Lord was not giving me any option.

Somehow, I knew that God was going to give me an answer about China that night. *Great,* I thought. *I'm going to get a big red light saying "Stop," and I'll be able to go back to bed and sleep peacefully.*

Creeping quietly out of bed to avoid waking Julie, I dressed, grabbed my glasses, and tiptoed out the door. When I arrived, I was still unsure what God intended me to do. I sat at my desk and decided the best place to start was in the Bible.

At that time, I'd been studying the Psalms daily, so I turned to the one next in line, Psalm 37:

*Fret not thyself because of evildoers, neither be
thou envious against the workers of iniquity. For
they shall soon be cut down like the grass, and
wither as the green herb. Trust in the Lord, and do
good; so shalt thou dwell in the land, and verily
thou shalt be fed. Delight thyself also in the Lord;
and he shall give thee the desires of thine heart.
Commit thy way unto the Lord; trust also in him;
and he shall bring it to pass.*

Then it hit me. I wasn't supposed to "fret" about
"evildoers," for they would "soon be cut down like
the grass." *Lord, are you telling me that Chairman Mao and these other "evil" guys are going to
fall? Lin Piao, Chou En Lai, the lot?*

With unquestionable conviction, I picked up a
pen and wrote at the side of the Psalm, "Mao
falls." Then I added the year *1969* to remind me of
the time God had "told" me. As I read on about
"dwelling in the land," it seemed clear to me that
when Mao died, God was going to open up China.

Next morning, I shared my experience with my
prayer partner, and then with Rip Carlson, the
business manager of the printshop. "I believe
God has given me His answer to my first question. I truly believe China will open up, but not
until Mao has fallen."

Rip, as always, listened with understanding. "I
agree. That sounds like God's voice to me also.
But what about your second question?"

"I don't know. I have no leading on that at all."

"David," he leaned across the desk, "read
Acts 26. You'll get it there."

I knew Rip. He was a man who walked very
close to the Lord; I respected him too much to
argue. As I opened the chapter, verse sixteen
came alive for me:

*But rise and stand upon your feet; for I have
appeared to you . . . to serve and bear witness to*

the things in which you have seen me and to those in which I will appear to you. . . .

Was I being called to witness to the "things which I had seen" last night? I read on to verses 17 and 18:

. . . delivering you from the people and from the Gentiles—to whom I send you to open their eyes, that they may turn from darkness to light and from the power of Satan to God, that they may receive forgiveness of sins and a place among those who are sanctified by faith in me.

Yes, I could see that the people of China lived in darkness—Mao's darkness. But what could *I* do to open their eyes? My mind flashed quickly over my life, especially at the academic failures I'd experienced.

Despite these negative thoughts, I proceeded to complete my out-of-the-ordinary Bible study, ending with verse nineteen: "*Wherefore, O King Agrippa, I was not disobedient to the heavenly vision. . . .*"

There it was. My place was not to question my own qualifications or ability. All I had to do was to make sure I was not disobedient to the "vision" before me. God would do the rest.

That day I "bore witness" to that "vision" with several other colleagues. We sent a letter about China to Bob Bowman, the FEBC president in the United States.

His return letter gave us enthusiastic endorsement to put out a newsletter entitled, "China Will Open Soon. Are You Ready?" Copies of it circulated among the Chinese community of Manila. While funds were raised for the printing of the Gospels, our small group pooled our savings to finance a research trip to the Chinese borders.

The journey was timed to coincide with my next liaison trip to Vietnam. In that September of 1969, I also took additional trips to Laos, Burma, Cambodia, and Hong Kong. I wanted to seek out what we termed "depositories," people who would store Bibles for the future when it would be possible to take them into China.

On my trip, I saw Burma as a key country with an important route into China through an isolated mountain range. I suspected that pathway might be ideal for Bible couriers. At the time, however, Westerners could enter Burma for only twenty-four hours.

Having gotten its independence from Britain in 1948, the country had soon closed up with the Marxist-tinted Burmese version of socialism. In 1965, the government was toppled by a military coup. The present government was atheistic, yet afraid of the religious leaning of the people.

Its twenty-four-hour restriction, however, left me very little time to search out both depositories and mountain passes. I wondered how I would manage to achieve my goals, little suspecting that the same Lord who had proven faithful so many times previously, had this problem in hand too.

Shortly before my planned visit I applied for my visa in the Burmese Embassy of another country. The girl behind the counter checked my documents closely. Then, looking up at me with a smile, she casually asked, "Would you like a visa for seventy-two hours?"

I did a double take. "Is that possible?" I said, trying to restrain my excitement.

"Yes, sir, we have a new policy for foreign visitors. You can now stay for up to three days."

Seventy-two hours. That was more than enough time to accomplish all my plans.

"When did your government introduce this new law?" I asked her.

"Yesterday," she smiled. "You're the first foreigner to make use of it. Will it be seventy-two then?"

I nodded absently, all the while marveling at God whose caring provision I was only just beginning to discover.

On my first night in Burma, I looked out of my bedroom window from the Christian home I was visiting. I stared at the impressive building opposite me. A red flag with five golden stars fluttered outside it in the cool breeze.

My heart seemed to skip a beat, as I realized what was before me—the Embassy of the People's Republic of China.

As hoped, Rangoon, Burma, did indeed provide me with key Christian contacts, willing to store Bibles for future delivery to China. And those contacts confirmed the suitability of the mountain route for transporting Bibles!

FIVE
PROVISIONS, PROVISIONS

"Honey, you've just got to read this book!" Julie thrust a paperback into my hands. "It's the story of a guy who's done everything you're talking about."

But I wasn't very interested because of my long-standing reading problem. I read through a book at a snail's pace. When I saw this one, in small type, and over 200 pages long, I winced.

God's Smuggler. The title sounded promising. I scanned the blurb . . . interesting. I devoured the book in four days—a record for me! I was especially thrilled by the chapter about the author's trip to China. Julie was right. This man, with his work in Europe, had done all that I longed to do in China.

Then, shortly after my trip to China's borders, an airmail letter arrived from Holland. The address was unfamiliar. The letter read:

Dear Brother David,
While passing through Saigon and Bangkok recently, I heard your name in connection with your recent trip to Burma. As you can imagine, I was deeply interested and very much wanted to see you. . . . Please continue the good work, and let us pray that we can meet soon and discuss the work of getting Scriptures into Red China.
> *Yours in the wonderful battle,*
> *Brother Andrew*

I couldn't believe it! This was the very person whose book I'd just read, and here was a letter from him encouraging *me*. Later, I discovered that he had been traveling with Corrie ten Boom, whose book *The Hiding Place* describes her World War II work with the Jews. The two of them had passed through the same countries I had just visited, but in the opposite direction. During the trip, some Wycliffe missionaries with whom I'd made contact had related my burden to get Bibles into China.

Julie and I both agreed I should accept Brother Andrew's amazing invitation to Holland. The best time would be our upcoming furlough. But we had no money for the ticket. FEBC didn't either. All they could provide was the money for me to attend a Christian literature conference in Chicago—as their representative.

While I did my best to express thanks for that, I couldn't resist again sharing why I believed the Lord wanted me to visit Holland.

"I, too, can see God may be in this, David," FEBC's president said. "If the Lord brings the money to you, then you have my permission to go. But *He* must be the one to supply it. You're not to ask anyone."

"I'll let you know what happens," I said with a grin.

"Meanwhile, enjoy yourself in Chicago," he said, shaking my hand.

The conference was attended by gifted men and women at the top of their fields in Christian literature work within their respective organizations. Though sent to represent FEBC, I felt out of my depth before this impressive group.

Yet, at the same time, I knew God had brought me into that situation. And I knew I had to share my burden for China.

I thus included our plans for China in my report on FEBC's current work. Up until the moment I mentioned China, everyone had nodded approvingly. But as I described our vision for Bible distribution inside the People's Republic, I watched a cloud of doubt descend on the faces of the participants.

I couldn't blame them. At that time, China was at the zenith of the Cultural Revolution. Violent persecution was "purging" the nation of all dissident elements. Mao's Little Red Book was studied daily with a fervor hardly to be found even among Christians in Bible study.

No one present seemed to consider China a mission field anymore. Without logic or data, I couldn't convince them of the possibility of Scripture distribution there. "China is closed," they told me. "What is the sense in spending time, effort, and money on China at the moment? Someday, perhaps, when it opens up, when the climate shifts. . . ."

I agreed. It did seem impossible, even crazy, to be looking toward China at such a time. I couldn't see how God was going to open the way for such a ministry either. But at that moment, the words of old Mr. Roy, my counselor, came back to me: "We're not called to 'see,' Son. We're called to obey the voice of the Lord. Paul says ours is a walk of faith, not sight."

Whether or not it made sense from a human perspective, I was convinced, beyond the shadow of a doubt, that the China work was a task God had set before me. And I had to get on with it.

That same voice of conviction was also urging me to trust for the money to visit Brother Andrew. Again, if I looked at things logically, it made no sense at all. I had only enough money to take me to New York, with a mere fifty dollars over, but that would not fly me very far across the Atlantic.

Still, if the Lord was the one urging me, then He would have to provide the rest of the money. With the reassurance of John 15:7, "If you abide in me, and my words abide in you, ask whatever you will, and it shall be done for you," I decided to go ahead with plans for the trip.

Before flying to Holland, I had scheduled several days visiting two old friends on the East Coast. The first was Neil McKinnon, a Scottish-born, retired missionary to the Philippines.

I told him about the changes in the direction of the FEBC press and shared the China vision. Neil was sympathetic. I explained that I was on my way to meet Brother Andrew in Holland.

"How are you getting there, David? Who is paying the bill?"

"The Lord is taking me there," I said. "I'm not allowed to ask for help from anybody. So it has to be God who meets the cost."

"And how close are you to taking the trip?" Neil asked.

"Well, I have thirty-five dollars in my pocket." Fifteen dollars had already gone in living expenses. "After seeing you, I'm going back to New York to visit other friends, the Olsen family. From there I'm flying back to L.A. to see Julie and the three D's. And . . ." I stopped. Even though I already had a ticket for Los Angeles, the prospect of lasting out the week in Washington and New York on thirty-five dollars was dismal.

Making that trip to Holland seemed an impossibility.

Neil grinned. "Dave, you're incurable."

"You don't believe in miracles?" I asked.

Neil chuckled. "Sure, I believe. What do you think I'm grinning about? Listen to this. Someone has gone and booked you for four days at the Washington Hilton, all expenses paid, to attend a fellowship conference with me before you leave."

"You're kidding."

"I'm not. Keep your thirty-five dollars, man. It

might take you to Holland yet." Neil and I never found out who it was that shouldered my expenses.

On the third morning of the conference, I was in the elevator on my way down for breakfast when two ladies got on. The older of the two gave a start as soon as she set eyes on me. I was not sure if I knew her from way back, so to play safe, I said "hello." She didn't reply and didn't stop staring. It was getting uncomfortable. Finally, like one awakened from a deep sleep, she opened her purse, rummaged through it, and brought out some bills.

"Excuse me, sir," she said. "We don't know each other, but the Spirit of the Lord is telling me right now to give you all the money in my purse. Here it is." She handed me twelve dollars.

Completely stunned, I could barely stammer out my thanks. This lady later became a regular supporter of the church in China.

On the fourth evening of the conference, I went to a crowded late-night prayer meeting. Towards the end, an old black woman in her eighties stood up and said, "The Lord is speaking to me and telling me to speak a word to some of you here."

The gray-haired lady, her face radiant, moved around the room. When she got to Neil, she said, "Brother, the Lord is telling me that He has called you into a ministry with young people." Besides me, Neil had told no one that he had been praying about returning to the United Kingdom to engage in youth work there.

Later, she moved in my direction. I was feeling rather embarrassed about this kind of meeting, and at one time even contemplated leaving the room. I'd never seen anything like it; the whole scene was somewhat disconcerting to me.

Finally, she stood in front of me. I knew that she and the others had no idea about my burden for the People's Republic. "Young man, I have something to say to you, too. The Lord is telling me that you're going to be involved in a ministry to China."

I was amazed and deeply encouraged since I was still a long way from my trip to Holland, let alone Bible distribution behind the Bamboo Curtain. I was grateful for the confirmation that I was heading in the *right* direction after all.

After the conference I left Washington twelve dollars richer and headed for New York City to see my other friends, the Olsens. I had come to know this family five years earlier in New York when I was being trained to use specialized equipment for FEBC.

At that time, I had gone trusting God to somehow provide money for an extended stay in a hotel. I'd met the Olsens outside on the snow-covered sidewalk of the church I'd just attended. Although I'd mentioned nothing about my needs, they had invited me to stay with their family for the duration of my training. They had a special "missionary room" reserved in their house.

Later, I discovered this godly family of Eastern European immigrants had been featured in David Wilkerson's book *The Cross and the Switchblade,* though, at the time, I had never even heard of the book. They were working in his Teen Challenge rehabilitation program among the teenage slum dwellers of New York.

Every night of my stay with them, I saw one scene repeated consistently. As soon as dinner and the clean-up were over, Mother Olsen would kneel beside an old leather chair near the fireplace. For as many as five hours she would pray for each of her eight children and also for God's work in the United States and around the world. Later, many of her children went into full-time work for the Lord. One of them, Amo, began a ministry among Jewish people called "Bless Israel Today."

So, now, after five years I had the privilege of seeing them again. My knock brought Marie, one of their daughters, to the door. "David!" she shrieked. I took a step forward, expecting a warm greeting and an invitation inside. Instead, she did an about-turn and left me standing in the cold. Then, just as mysteriously, she returned and handed me an envelope.

"Open it," she urged with a secret smile. The envelope was addressed to me. Inside was $300!

I stood on the doorstep, unable to speak or to tear my eyes away from the money. It was exactly what I needed to get across the Atlantic and back.

Marie's happy laughter pealed out. "Well, don't just stand there. Thank the Lord."

"Thank you, Lord!" I exclaimed fervently, and then threw back my head to laugh from sheer joy. From various parts of the house, the other Olsens came running to greet me. My boisterous joy had announced my arrival.

Later, over coffee and sandwiches, Marie told me God had directed her to save part of her tithe for me ever since the day we had left for Manila. She was not sure how much she was going to give me. "But you will step in one day, and whatever sum is in the envelope on that day is the right sum for you." It was the exact amount I needed. Hello, Holland! Hello, Brother Andrew!

I knew without question that the Lord was leading me to Holland. And His faithful provision was taking me every inch of the way.

SIX
THE DUTCH CONNECTION

On March 2, 1970, I stepped from the plane onto Dutch soil. George, a member of Brother Andrew's staff, met me at Schipol Airport. I expected to be driven directly to Brother Andrew's home in Ermelo about fifty miles away. Instead, George drove me south of Amsterdam to a friend's house in a village near the coast.

"We're treating you to dinner. Dutch treat," George explained, but caught himself. "No, I mean this is on us, but the treat is typically Dutch!"

I was intrigued, of course.

"Ah! We've been expecting you, David. Come in!" Three gentlemen greeted me at the door. The spokesman for the group continued, "I am Peter van Dyke, your host for the day. The gentleman with curly hair is Jan, and that one with the moustache is Johan." Mr. van Dyke led me inside as he talked. "We're Brother Andrew's welcoming committee. You must be famished. Come. Dinner's been waiting for the past thirty minutes!"

We gathered around the dining table with a beautiful setting of bone china, crystal, silverware, and tulips. "Lord," my host prayed, "thank you for our brother's safe trip and this chance to fellowship with him. Thank you also for this wonderful Dutch dinner of raw herring and raw onions. May it nourish his body as well as it has nourished Dutch bodies since the birth of the Dutch nation, in Jesus' Name we pray. Amen."

My ears twitched. Raw herring and what?

Alarmed, I opened my eyes. Right in front of me was a crystal platter brimming with raw herring and raw onion rings.

"Amen," I gulped audibly. I watched them cut off the tail and debone the herring. Then laying the raw clammy fish on a piece of rye, they slapped two thick onion rings over it. I meekly accepted one of these from my host and watched as the other men hungrily devoured their servings. I opened my mouth to follow suit and prayed. With each bite I prayed harder.

The four Dutchmen watched me casually. One of them caught my eye and smiled. A nervous grin distorted my features until I had carefully swallowed every bit down. Instantly, the four Dutchmen gave me a standing ovation. "Congratulations. Marvelous!"

Mr. van Dyke scratched his head. "You're something! You're the first non-Dutchman who did it. I thought Americans hated raw fish and raw onions."

"You'd better believe it. We hate it! I did it for you. If you want to know the truth, I asked the Lord to help me through every last mouthful." All five of us bellowed with laughter. It had been a test, from beginning to end.

"Now our American brother deserves to eat the rest of the dinner," Mr. van Dyke announced, as the cook brought in a hot thick soup and a juicy pot roast. They were delicious!

"I hear you've already had one of our herrings," Brother Andrew said when he stepped into the office. I looked into the face of a man I knew smiled easily. The laugh lines around his eyes and mouth had become a permanent fixture.

He was slim and neatly dressed. Though humble and gentle-looking, he had an inner strength and courage which overwhelmed me.

56

This was the famous "smuggler" whose life and work for the Lord had been written up into a best-seller. I was tongue-tied in his presence.

But not for long. During the days we spent together, I felt very much at home with this concerned Dutchman. I showed him the Psalms which I'd marked in my Bible, and the "Call to China" written in the margin near Acts 26. I explained my vision for getting Scriptures into the hands of the Chinese. After the skepticism which had greeted me elsewhere, my spirit soared as he nodded in agreement.

When I described my visits to countries bordering China, he responded in an earnest tone. "Brother David, that's not enough. You need to go yourself. I had American and Taiwanese visas in my passport and still I got in. If God wants you in, He'll open the door for you to go through."

Then, with a twinkle in his eye, he added, "I believe the door is already open."

Later, he shared with me his experiences in China. People just weren't interested in any Bibles. The one church he had been able to locate in Beijing (Peking) discouraged him almost as much as the indifference he found on the streets. And what he found were very old people in a barren little building used as a church; all had nodded off to sleep during the sermon.

"If this represented Chinese Christianity, I realized their government could stamp it out overnight if it wanted to."

So, was the Church in China really dead?

Certainly, to the outside world, it seemed that public religious activity, Christian, Muslim, or Buddhist, had all but disappeared in China since the Cultural Revolution. Churches, mosques, monasteries, and temples everywhere had been looted and then closed. Many had become factories, warehouses, movie theatres, and meeting halls; others had been simply locked and left derelict.

"David, I believe the Lord would have you seek out the Church in China. In fact, you need to go on what I like to term a 'seek and save' mission."

"What do you mean by a 'seek and save' mission?" I asked.

His face clouded. "On last year's trip into Vietnam, I read an article in an American newspaper which disturbed me deeply. It was one of those reports on the war in Vietnam that used a military expression I had not heard before: 'search and destroy.' It got such a hold of me I felt like weeping. Corrie ten Boom was traveling with me, and she read the article too. Afterwards she quoted the very words I had been thinking of.

"'"Search and destroy,"' Corrie mused. 'It's just the opposite of what Jesus said.' Then she cited Jesus' description of the reason for His coming. '"I am come to seek and to save that which was lost."'

Brother Andrew concluded, "In that war-like situation, where 'search and destroy' had become a watchword, our job surely was to 'seek and save,' and do what Jesus did.

"Brother David, I believe you should find the church in China. Locate it. Help it. Encourage it. Feed it. Love it."

In the cold crisp mornings before breakfast, I often sat by the small window of my room and watched Brother Andrew's family working in the garden. I saw the famous "Bible-smuggler" wearing his traditional wooden clogs as he tended the beans, potatoes, and other vegetables.

Sometimes, he would stop to help his five children care for their animals. While the young girls were busy with the rabbits, the boys took care of the chickens and goats.

As I watched this laughing, loving family, they

would occasionally wave at me and grin. I knew that Brother Andrew enjoyed nothing more than being with his wife and family. Both he and I really had a lot in common. We both loved our families and home. Both of us had been in the armed services—Andrew in the Army, I in the Marines. And both of us shared the same burden for the church in China.

I felt a God-given bond with this man as we prepared to ally in the spiritual battle in those atheistic countries where Satan had established a stranglehold. Indeed, not only had the devil established a grip on these nations, it seemed that he had set up a counterfeit religion as well.

One afternoon, I listened as Brother Andrew explained his fascinating view of communism as a religion.

"At the end of my trip to China," he said, "I sat next to an English woman on the flight out of the country. Almost the first thing she said to me was, 'How can any nation survive without faith in God, without an object of worship?'

"'But they do have one,' I told her. 'They have Mao.' That set me thinking: How many elements of religion is communism emulating on a world-wide basis?

"Every communist country I can think of has an object of worship. Even in Moscow, they have the mausoleum in Red Square. I have seen the extreme devotion of the people lining up to pay homage to Lenin.

"But that's not all. Communism takes other religious guises as well. For example, it often finds an enemy. You must know what you stand against in a religion, and China's substitute for that right now is America, the 'Paper Tiger.' When there is no visible enemy on the outside, they create one on the inside, and I believe that is part of the reason for the Cultural Revolution. That's why there are continuous purges in communism. That, of course, fits their basic concept of continuous struggle, continuous revolution.

"Another major element they copy is the need for a holy book. In Europe, it is the Communist Manifesto, and in China—Mao's own Little Red Book.

"The fourth aspect is more subtle than these. All around the world, religions have a martyr figure, and no doubt the communists see Jesus in just such a role. Of course, that isn't fair. Martyrs are men who die for a cause and *stay dead*. Jesus has overcome death for all time. He is the Resurrection and the Life! But all the same, they like to copy.

"So many communists make a big deal of their countrymen who have died 'for the cause,' and then set them up as heroes for their people. That is why I am against military invasion of communist countries. The more you fight communism that way, the more martyrs you supply them with, and the more you strengthen their cause."

His final point was that communism, like all religions, had its own promise for the future. "They don't proclaim the life hereafter, but they look to the 'heaven on earth' their philosophy will bring. That's why no country in the world claims to be communistic. They all say, 'We are socialistic,' and socialism is a stepping stone to communism. Communism can only be realized when the new man has emerged out of the new society. That new humanity is the great hope for the future and the goal of their efforts."

"So that makes communism a carbon copy of religion in general," I said, as he finished.

"Sure," he replied. "Communists are not fools. They know man is looking for something greater than himself. They try to feed their people this way to keep them quiet."

The picture was coming clear for me. "No wonder they're so frightened of Christianity."

"Yes. And no wonder so many people living under communism are looking for something more. Do you know, Brother David, there are strong elements of Christian revival in Russia today?"

"You've got to be joking."

"Not at all. The people are fed up with a counterfeit religion. Now they are after the real thing." His voice was earnest. "I just pray that will soon be the case in China too, as the people have time to become disenchanted with what their government is offering them.

"I believe it is possible, David. More than that, I am sure it will happen. It has to. And do you know the craziest part of all?" he continued in a subdued tone. "These so-called world powers think they are masterminding the whole operation. But even *they* are being deceived! There is another power working behind them, whose purposes they don't even realize they are fulfilling.

"It is the Devil himself. Who else would try so hard to spread atheism in every country of the world?

"But Satan is stupid!" He laughed. "He is trying hard to win the battle himself, yet the very system he is propagating is leaving the people so hungry they are turning back to the Lord in greater numbers than ever!"

During our time together, we spent hours talking, praying and sharing the Scriptures. Toward the end, I showed him Mark 10:13, which had challenged me to *publish* the gospel abroad.

"David, what are you really thinking about in terms of Bibles?" Brother Andrew asked.

"I'm praying with my friends in Manila for ten million Scriptures for China."

I'd said it.

Now I waited to see whether this man, like so many others, would laugh at such an idea. I almost regretted telling him.

"Well, from our perspective that may sound like a lot of Bibles," he began. "But I'm sure in God's eyes it's not so many. Anyway, it's only one-fourth of one percent of the Chinese population."

His eyes were bright with enthusiasm. "If we can't trust the Lord for such a tiny proportion, we can't trust Him for anything. I stand with you in that vision, David."

"How can we work together?" I asked Brother Andrew.

I told him that within FEBC I could work the presses, just as we had for so many other organizations. His role would be to share his experiences of crossing communist borders in Eastern Europe.

"You are the one who can show us how to get into closed countries," I said.

"No, you're wrong, David. China is *not* closed. No country is closed. The Bible says, 'I have set before you an open door which no man can shut.' All we have to do is obey the Lord, go, and He will show where that open door is."

I left Holland excited. Somewhere there was a way to get Bibles inside China. It was time for us to find it. And the sooner, the better!

SEVEN

MUSHROOMS, PEANUTS, AND WATERMELONS

On my return to Los Angeles, I shared my visit to Brother Andrew with the FEBC team. I also made clear our mutual conviction that a Bible ministry inside China was possible. Despite my eagerness to begin a ministry to China, FEBC had other plans for our American furlough: They wanted me to organize an evangelistic campaign for young people in my old home town in California, much as Robert Foster and I had done in Manila.

It was the last thing I'd expected. Nevertheless, I tried hard to be patient about my plans for China and plunged into the youth campaign as enthusiastically as I could.

Without a doubt God blessed the campaign. Ralph Bell, from the Billy Graham team, riveted the audience's attention with his message. Andrae Crouch and "Love Song" backed up his words with powerful music. We thanked God as 1,500 people came to Jesus. It was a good time, even a great time.

But it wasn't China. And that country continued tugging at my heartstrings. "Perhaps now, Lord," I prayed after the final youth meeting. "Will I be able to do something for China now?"

No. My next task with FEBC was to work on equipment at Station KGER in San Mateo, California. The need was urgent, requiring immediate attention.

"I'll be gone only a week, Honey," I assured Julie. Doing my best to put on a brave front, I inwardly resented the assignment. I'd already spent many weeks, without getting closer to meeting the needs of China. I was angry and frustrated.

The "week" in San Mateo became a month, followed by a second one. After three months, Julie and the kids came to live with me. The end of the job was nowhere in sight. Neither was the People's Republic of China.

By now, the resentment had almost taken me over completely. This task not only had nothing to do with China, but in addition, many well-meaning friends had advised me to drop my Chinese "pipe-dreams."

Another six months dragged by slowly. I knew I had become chained to my frustration. Despite Julie's gentle encouragement to hand it to the Lord for Him to solve, I couldn't. Or rather, I wouldn't.

My spiritual life was at an all-time low. One Sunday morning I turned on the T.V. and heard a preacher talking about harboring bitterness. His words seemed directed at me.

"Even now, in your home, if God is speaking to you, why don't you bring your resentment out into the open? Lay it all before Him. Ask His forgiveness and begin life anew." I knew I had to pray that prayer for myself. As I did, I found myself relaxing for the first time in months. I had a new peace when I set out for work the next morning.

At work, I was told there was a new job for me. I'd be working with Jack Hill in Sacramento, California, taking down five radio towers.

"Where will they be going?"

"Once you've got them down, we'll ship them to an island in South Korea. From there, we'll be using them to beam gospel programs into Red China."

The Lord had me back working for China again,

once I'd let go of my resentment. It had been that simple.

My job was to drill 5,800 holes into the dismantled towers to prepare them for galvanization. Potentially, it was one of the dreariest assignments imaginable: Standing and sweating in the hot sun of California's capital city, while drilling hole after hole for three long weeks. Yet it was for the Chinese that Jack and I would be working. My spirit soared in that knowledge.

"Lord Jesus," I prayed each time I drilled, "for this hole I'm going to trust You for a thousand souls in China."

I repeated the prayer 5,800 times during the three weeks it took to complete my task. I was literally drilling for China.

Step number two toward China followed a few days later with word that Brother Andrew had been trying to make contact with me again. He was concerned because he hadn't heard anything from me for months.

He also sent me a ticket to meet him for a one-day stopover at JFK Airport in New York. As I told him what had happened, he listened sympathetically. "I had no idea all this was going on, David. I thought you had just been too busy to write."

The past behind us, we spent that twenty-four hours looking to the future. We prayed together, planned together, and discussed our goals of penetrating China with Bibles.

There was one brick wall we always came up against: Even when the "smuggler" himself had managed to get Bibles into China, nobody there would accept them. Why? The reason was simple. The only reading allowed in China at that time was Mao's Little Red Book, or a narrow selection of other writings, equally political in style. It was impossible for the people to accept anything looking like a Bible.

How could we overcome that problem? We prayed until the Lord finally broke through our frustration. Why couldn't we print our New Testaments to look precisely like Mao's famous book?

"I can see it now," smiled Brother Andrew. "Everyone carrying them up and down the streets will look like dedicated supporters of the Revolution. But, in fact, they will be holding the Word of God."

I was equally excited. "I can easily get hold of one of Mao's books. And we'll copy it down to the final detail. Our New Testament will be the same size, same color, and have an identical cover."

I left Brother Andrew that day with an order for 25,000 of the most unusual New Testaments we were ever to print at FEBC.

Our furlough in America over, my family and I would be returning to our work at the Philippine base of FEBC, and I was looking forward to the months ahead. Top of the list was the order that had been placed by Brother Andrew for 25,000 New Testaments. And there was only one machine which was adequate to handle this particular order—the Fairchild ColorKing, the one I had asked the Lord about that night more than two years before.

The next few months were very busy. I had a new peace as I bustled about the press, doing the work which I knew God wanted us to do. We were printing Bibles; we were ministering to China. The two were united now, and would be united for a long time at FEBC.

Still, I felt an inner tugging to follow the China ministry even farther, yet I couldn't see the next step ahead.

The Lord had one more step of preparation for me to take, another lesson for me to learn. Without it, I would never have been in a position to trust Him for a mission field the size of the People's Republic of China.

That lesson came through a hair-brained scheme for an FEBC multi-media project, dreamed up by Pablo, one of my co-workers, along with Todd Martin, our communications man, and my old drilling companion, Jack Hill.

Out on the field for FEBC, Pablo and Todd had researched the potential listening audience of FEBC's Manila market. They discovered that most of the city's population was under age thirty and had a major drug problem.

They planned a top-forty program broadcasting from a secular rock station. In addition, a newspaper would be prepared, having the gospel message in a readable format for young people. A good quality Christian film and a top Christian music group would also be part of the multi-media approach.

Despite reservations at first, I too caught their vision and got involved in the planning and prayer sessions. We were wondering where the $15,000 in U.S. currency needed to air the show was going to come from.

"Sponsors!" I called out. "We can get a couple of multi-national companies to support us. They'll never miss the money."

I was elected to make the contacts, and the reception I got seemed very positive. We just had to hear the word from the main company headquarters in the States. The answer was "no."

"But, sir, didn't you say...?" I groped for words.

"I said 'yes' as far as I was concerned. But the States thought differently."

"May I ask why?"

"Well, to be quite frank, their actual words were:

'These people are offering us a peanut, and asking for a watermelon in return!' "

We'd been expecting sponsors to carry us through financially. We realized we had been depending more on them than on the Lord. As we prayed asking for forgiveness, we turned the success of the plan over to Him completely.

Within a few days, the Lord actually provided us with another pair of sponsors and our program went on the air. It rose to number one among the secular stations and met the needs of many hundreds of young people who phoned in special requests for counseling.

Eventually we showed *The Cross and the Switchblade* movie to a total of one-fourth of a million people in Manila. More than 14,000 people expressed a desire to commit their lives to Christ.

"The whole thing's blowing my mind," I said at one of our prayer times. "In my wildest dreams I never dared hope it would get so big."

Todd Martin responded, "You know when all this started? The moment we realized it was crazy to put our hopes on anything but God. That was the turning point."

He was right.

"It's like a mushroom cloud," mused Pablo. "The whole thing started out so small, and just expanded from that little bit of faith we had to begin with."

"You know what else it's like?" I asked with a chuckle. "It's as though we gave the Lord a peanut of faith, and He gave us back a whole *field* full of watermelons!"

But the show wasn't over yet. An even bigger step was waiting for me. "Love Song," the famous gospel group, and its manager Mike MacIntosh, an ex-drug addict, had accepted our invitation to play in Manila. They would hold massive outdoor concerts for young people throughout the city.

President Marcos had now declared martial law, forbidding public gatherings of any size in Manila. But the "Love Song" concert proved the exception. It was the very first public meeting held at that time, and as a result, crowds of young people turned up. Some smoked pot, others drank beer, but all of them were willing to pay to hear Christian music. Eighty-five percent of the audience was non-Christian.

On the third night Mike MacIntosh followed the songs with a personal account of how Jesus had delivered him from drugs and restored his marriage. Out of the 15,000 gathered, 5,000 came forward to receive Christ.

After that experience, I expressed my feelings of gratitude for the way the Lord had worked above and beyond our efforts.

"Praise the Lord!" Robert Foster, my long-time prayer partner at FEBC, said when I told him about the 5,000 who'd responded to the MacIntosh message. "But the meetings are *over*. What's next? Where do you go from here?"

"China." My reply was immediate. "China's the next step." Then I stopped, realizing I hadn't planned on saying those words. Where on earth had they come from? The Lord?

I pondered the question for several days. The printing of 25,000 New Testaments for Brother Andrew had been completed, and those books had been moved to the borders of China. Work at FEBC was ahead of production. The six-month youth ministry project had been completed.

Maybe now, with extra time on my hands, I could be doing more for China. Was this why the Lord had been teaching me the "Mushroom Principle"—that with one small step of faith, taken in obedience, I could rely on God to do the impossible? And trust Him for something much bigger—like the impenetrable land of China?

"Lord, what do you want me to do?" I asked, as I agonized over the decision. I knew we were at a crossroad, but I didn't know which road was right. "I'll follow you, Lord, but please show me."

In a time like this, I'd gotten into the habit of reading the Bible, so I picked mine up and turned to Isaiah. For seven long hours, I alternately studied several chapters in Isaiah and waited on the Lord in prayer. Long after midnight, as I was reading chapter 42, the words came booming off the page:

I am the Lord, I have called you in righteousness, I have taken you by the hand and kept you, I have given you as a covenant to the people, a light to the nations, to open the eyes that are blind, to bring out the prisoners from the dungeon, from the prison those who sit in darkness.

Basically, I knew this was a prophetic passage about the coming Messiah. But in the context of the decision which I had put before the Lord, those words came alive for me in a second sense as well. These verses could precisely describe a ministry to China. Could this be it? Was this what God was saying to me?

"Please, Lord," I whispered, "I want to know for sure." I loved being at FEBC. We had very good friends on the compound, and I had no wish to step out of the warmth of that security into the cold unknown.

Besides, full-time work for China would be hard. "Lord, You know I don't have all the learning and the skills to handle this kind of complex job. If *You* want me to take it on, then You'll have to help me. Do You want me to leave FEBC?"

Immediately, the words of verse 9 hit me:

Behold, the former things have come to pass, and new things I now declare; before they spring forth, I tell you of them.

I grasped the message that I was not to cling to the former things, but to be prepared to accept the "new." The struggle was over. I knew what the Lord was telling me to do. And with that knowledge came a sense of quiet peace.

Julie smiled as she fixed me some tea and cookies. "To be honest, I've been expecting this, Dave—ever since you met Brother Andrew last year. I guessed it then."

"Guessed what?" After fourteen years of marriage, she still had surprises to spring.

"That you might leave FEBC to start the China ministry full-time."

"Why didn't you tell me?"

"Honey, it had to be the Lord, not me, who'd lead you in this."

The next day, I went to see Rip Carlson, the man who'd given me the verse in Acts 26 in 1969.

"I think you should work with Brother Andrew," he suggested. "After all, he did visit the States some time ago, asking FEBC for your services. You knew that, didn't you?"

I wrote to Brother Andrew right away. In a few weeks' time, he sent me a warm letter outlining the steps we should take to get the ministry started. Almost as a postscript, he added: "Welcome to the ministry." Now we'd be working together in earnest.

EIGHT
ON THE EDGE OF THE WORLD

No staff, no secretary, no office. Just Julie and me—and the Lord. But that was enough for the new ministry.

"David?" Julie called me one morning in April, four weeks into the new venture. "Remember Beng Tuazon? She's on the phone."

"Beng, how's everything?" I shouted. Beng had turned out to be a very lonely girl searching for herself and some true friends.

I remembered the first time Billy Wee, a Chinese friend, and I had met her. She was the sales and promotions manager for a big hotel in downtown Manila. "What can I do for you?" a baritone voice had belted out, impatiently. The voice was that of a man, but judging by the miniskirt, black stockings, earrings, long red fingernails, and low neckline, we knew we were dealing with a woman.

We'd come to get help lining up "Love Song." In spite of her thick make-up, false eyelashes, the cigarette dangling from her mouth, and the drink in one hand, Beng had been an enthusiastic supporter of "Love Song." She had provided them with seven rooms free, as well as a press conference, T.V. appearance, and a chance to play in a packed supper club.

Beng had been such a help. How could I not remember her! Now she was on the phone.

"Listen to this. I'm new. David, I've accepted Jesus Christ!" she said, excitedly.

After she said that, I noticed her happiness had

raised the key of her voice so that now she actually sounded like a girl.

"Why, Beng, praise the Lord! How'd it happen?"

"'Love Song' did it for me. A lot of young Filipinos were changed by that musical group. I've been seeing them. Say, listen to this. I saw slides of Brother Andrew's work at a youth conference. I even read his book there. Do you know, David, I've got a marvelous idea. I think I should join your new ministry . . . to help with all the office work. . . . I'm sure it's God's timing that I called!"

I wasn't as sure as she. I had no money to pay her. But she refused to listen to my excuses; she was prepared to live by faith.

"And don't you dare refuse God's grace," she told me. I didn't.

The change in this lady had been dramatic. The new Beng Tuazon who now uncomplainingly worked long hours without overtime pay had nothing in common with the "sophisticated hipster" I first met barely four months before.

Now I had a secretary, but no office. When I did get one, it too came in an unexpected way. After searching frequently in Manila's Chinatown, I found the perfect place in a small alleyway up on the fifteenth floor. It matched our needs and our budget perfectly.

The only problem was that Mr. Goh, the owner, wanted two months' rent in advance—and our bank balance was nil.

In any case, I felt an inner nudging that this was the office God meant us to have.

"Mr. Goh, I believe this is the place for our organization. But I don't have the money right now. If you'll excuse me, I'm going to lunch and will return with the money this afternoon."

Where the money was coming from, I had no idea. But if God really wanted me to have this office, He obviously knew something about how the money would come!

After lunch, before returning to Mr. Goh, I stopped to pick up my mail at the post office. There was only one letter—it was from Bill Windham, whom I'd worked with on the Ralph Bell Crusade in California years before. Besides a warm greeting, Bill had included a check. The amount precisely matched the rental fee!

I believe I flew, rather than walked, to Mr. Goh. Within minutes we had signed the contract together.

It was the same story again with the office furniture. I had spied a furniture store nearby and approached the manager, asking her to assess needs. To date, we had been working on wooden boxes.

She sized up the office and made her plans. It would all be ready in three weeks' time.

"I must point out that as yet we don't have any funds for it. But," I added hastily, "if you would be willing to trust God with me for the money, I believe it will have arrived here before you have finished the work."

"I am prepared to do that," she said graciously.

Her confidence took me by surprise. "Are you a Christian too, then?" I asked.

"No. I am a Buddhist."

"But you're willing to trust my God with me?"

"I am willing."

Three weeks later the furniture was ready. So was the money! Friends in Rolling Hills Estates in California had just deposited money into our near empty savings account. It more than covered the shopkeeper's bill.

During this time, however, we had one overriding concern with no obvious solution. We had to find a way to get someone into China to contact the Chinese believers, assess their needs, and to deliver God's Word into their hands.

I flew to Hong Kong to begin research among the Christians there. Many of them had come from the Mainland, and still had relatives living inside. Since FEBC also had a branch in Hong Kong, the Crown Colony, I decided to touch base with its staff during my stay.

When I arrived at the address, I was shocked to find that another Christian organization had taken its place. The secretary ushered me into the director's office.

Shan Kumar stood up to welcome me. Though not long, our visit was just enough to share ideas about an outreach to the Chinese. Originally of Eastern origin, Shan had worked in America with his evangelistic organization prior to his moving to Hong Kong. He was a highly educated man, with a deep grasp of a wide range of issues and a deep love for God.

I liked him immediately. I knew as we parted that I had met someone we could turn to for help in the future course of the ministry.

Though fruitful, the time of research in Hong Kong showed me one thing: As an American, I could fulfill only a part of the role required in this work. We simply had to find some Chinese Christians and work alongside them. Only when East and West worked hand in hand, could we truly know how best to serve the church in China.

Within a few weeks, I met the ones I had been praying for. Joseph Lee and his Uncle Liu had just returned from a trip to the Mainland where they had witnessed to their relatives about Jesus Christ. I was struck by the glow in their expressions. When we spoke of the need for the gospel in China, a wistful, far-off look of longing came over them, and I knew that both carried this burden very heavily.

We agreed to begin a four-month project together. They would spend three months in Hong Kong, asking the Christians there for contacts inside China. The final month would be a trip to the Mainland to deliver Bibles. At that time, it was easy for overseas Chinese to obtain visas to their homeland. For American "foreign devils" or *gwailos* like myself, it had so far proved impossible.

Their decision was a costly one. Both men could have been busy carving out a lucrative career in their family's business. But both had chosen a course which not only would pay them little in terms of salary, but also could endanger their freedom once they entered the People's Republic with Bibles.

While they sought for routes into China through its front door, I was searching for other openings through its back and side entrances. Thus began my travels to the borders of China's neighbors.

In Lahore, Pakistan, for example, I met a Christian who printed Bibles and was willing to send them to China through friends. "If you trust me," he said. Trust him! It would cost him his own life to get God's Word inside China, and he was willing to lay it down if necessary.

Within a few months, we began sending him Scriptures to deliver to Christian friends working along the borders. In turn, they passed them on to a believer who was a wireless operator in a nearby region. He then radioed friends who traveled from southern China to collect them.

Bibles began trickling their way into China from other remote countries, too. The 25,000 that FEBC had printed for Brother Andrew were slowly making their way past the country's boundaries. Nomads on mules or on foot would load their packs with as many Scriptures as they could carry and then travel enormous distances to their destinations. It was back-breaking work through dense jungles or over mountains in Burma, Nepal, Afghanistan, Pakistan, and every possible avenue into China.

One of the men who risked their lives to get Bibles to their people was Pastor Ling, a Chinese pastor who had been driven from his homeland. I first met him during a major meeting to plan Bible deliveries in Laos. Pastor Ling's face had an ugly, disfiguring scar. This old believer had obviously suffered heavily for his faith.

Without thinking, I reached out to shake his right hand. Instead, he offered his left. He had to. His right arm ended in a stump at his elbow. I embraced him, hating myself for being so unobservant.

Since that first meeting, he had been tireless in his commitment to organize Bible deliveries across the border. He had been personally responsible for a large proportion of the 25,000 we had delivered.

He seldom spoke of the persecution he had undergone; he was too busy speaking for the Lord. But one morning before I left Vientiane, he shared his story with me.

Trained in the China Inland Mission School in Hunan Province, he had soon become a pastor. "After the communists took control," he explained, "the missionaries were forced to leave, and I worked on my own with my 'flock.'"

In 1952, the communists put him in prison where he stayed until 1957. During that time his congregation faithfully prayed for his protection and release.

Pastor Ling returned to his home and continued preaching. Revival began to break out and word of it soon reached the ears of the authorities.

Once again he was dragged off to prison. This

time the senior officer personally dealt with him. He ordered Pastor Ling to be tied against a wall with his arms outstretched in a crucifixion pose. Two soldiers, sent to torture him, shouted angrily, "Fool! You haven't learned your lesson yet. You *must* learn it."

With that, one turned around the rifle he was holding and brought the butt down right across Pastor Ling's face from his nose to his jaw. The skin was peeled open and began to bleed profusely. The soldiers released him but not until they had cut off one of his arms at the elbow.

"I was imprisoned again," he concluded, "for just a few more years. Now I can only do my work here from Laos. But at least, I can get the Word in to continue 'feeding my sheep' that way."

His eyes had a distant look, as he gently smiled. "If the Lord should ask me to give my life for my people," he said softly, "I am ready."

I knew he meant it. Once again, I glanced at his scar and the stump of his arm. I wanted to echo his words. But I had never been in a position of choosing my life or my faith.

If that day ever came, could I know for sure how I would respond? Could I be certain I would pay the price?

There was another Chinese Christian Shan Kumar suggested I see while in the border countries. His name was Yan Chee, an evangelist among the Himalayans.

Forced in 1949 to flee Inner Mongolia with his family, Yan Chee had met Shan several years later. When I mentioned Shan's name, Yan Chee welcomed me warmly, even though my visit was unexpected.

"Brother David, would you allow me to share something with you? Something very close to my heart?" Yan Chee asked after some time together. "I want to start ministering to my own people again. And I know one way to do it. I believe God is telling me to start getting His Word to the Chinese across the border."

My mouth must have fallen open in surprise. So far during our hour-and-a-half visit, I had had no chance to explain the purpose of my visit. Now here was Yan Chee telling me what I had planned telling *him!*

"How would you get the Bibles inside?" I asked, having recovered from his disclosure.

"Oh, I know many ways through the mountains. The communist government need not know about them." Then, after pausing to smile, he said, "It is physically difficult to cross these mountains and that makes it safe from detection. I know people who will help me."

"Have you delivered any before?" I asked.

"Once. A friend gave me some Bibles that had recently been deposited here. They were nice ones—with red covers. And they looked just like Mao's book."

I knew the friend he meant. We had delivered some of the 25,000 to a European missionary in the area. By now, I was smiling broadly. "If someone provided you with all the Bibles you wanted, could you get them into China?"

"Certainly," Yan Chee responded. At that, I shook his hand.

"I am positive that God has brought us together," I said with obvious delight.

For about a week we spent time praying and planning strategy. I left him with the promise to give him Bibles which he said three men could deliver immediately.

That trek proved to be only the start of many long treks for him and his teams.

While on the borders, I had another task to fulfill. Brother Andrew had repeatedly stressed the need for me to get inside China myself. Every attempt I had made so far had met with dismal failure. I had visited a number of Chinese embassies in the border countries, but had always been turned down. However, on the final leg of my journey, I decided to try the embassy in Kathmandu.

"I'm a friend of the embassy people," I told the embassy guard who let me into the reception area. It was bare, except for a sofa, coffee table, two armchairs, and a partially empty magazine rack. Very quickly, I took some red-jacketed New Testaments from my pocket and slipped them into the magazine rack beside identical Mao books. Just in time. A gray-suited embassy official entered, smiling politely and somewhat warily.

"Yes, what can we do for you?"

"I'm interested in traveling into China."

"Please have some tea," he offered. We sat quietly for a few moments and sipped tea.

Since Nixon's much-heralded trip to China, my host was not surprised that an American wanted to visit China, too.

"You are a friend of our country?" he asked, after a period of silence.

"Oh, yes, your country is a favorite of mine. I love it. In fact, I have many Chinese friends," I replied.

The official smiled and we sipped more tea. He was very eager to chat since the embassy had very few guests and almost no foreign ones. When the time came for me to leave, he asked me to return for tea the next day. I, of course, accepted his gracious invitation.

The next day, I returned and was again taken to the reception room. I noticed the New Testaments had already been removed from the magazine rack. In a flash, I restocked the supply when no one was in the room and waited for the official.

Though my visa to China did not materialize as

a result of those visits, I wasn't disappointed. For the first time, I'd been able to sit alongside a Chinese communist and relate to him as a person, not as a cog in the giant party machinery. The man had responded to genuine friendship and had even betrayed a hint of loneliness.

With so much talk at that time of "Commie b____s" and the dreaded Red Peril, it had become easy for us in the West either to hate or to fear these people.

Jesus had not called us to do either. He had died for them just as He had for us. And He was calling us to love them. For His sake.

NINE

"DON'T GO TO CHINA—
IT'S DANGEROUS!"

The Star Ferry threw its engine noisily into reverse and pulled slowly into the terminal. A sea of hurrying passengers moved up the passageway and out into the streets of Hong Kong. In the crowd was Joseph, in his third month of searching among Chinese Christians for contacts in the Mainland.

"Hey, Joseph. Wait!" The voice was that of a friend from one of Hong Kong's Bible colleges. "What brings you here?" he asked Joseph as the two began walking with the jostling crowd.

"My uncle and I are going to China again," Joseph replied.

The man stared in disbelief. Then grasping his arm, he quickly pulled Joseph away from the crowd. "I must warn you. Don't go to China. It's dangerous!"

Though young and inexperienced, Joseph was still aware of the dangers involved. He had hoped to find help and support from this Bible scholar, but all he could read in the man's eyes and voice were fear and concern.

I must be crazy wanting to go into China. I may not even be able to get out again, he thought after the two had parted. *Is it fair to my family to take this risk? Am I sensible to enter a hostile land in search of a people who are not legally recognized as existing anyway?*

His friend's advice was typical of the comments Joseph and Uncle Liu had encountered already in

Hong Kong. In fact, no Chinese Christians had even been willing to give them the names of believers to visit in China.

Despite their disappointment, the two men could understand the cold wall of silence which had greeted their inquiries.

Since the Cultural Revolution in 1966, the "Great Helmsman," Chairman Mao, had made a vicious purge of "dissident" elements in China; those included the Christian churches. Actual suffering of believers in China dated almost as far back as the communist take-over in 1949. During a brief two-year "honeymoon" period in which the worst evils of the old society disappeared, Christians had continued worshiping. Many missionaries had even stayed to carry on with their work.

By 1951, however, the Three-Self Patriotic Movement had been organized. Its origins lay in a meeting between the "Church of Christ" and Chou En-Lai, held the previous year. From that conference emerged both the "Christian Manifesto," a required admission that the church had been used as a tool of imperialism in China, and a pledge of allegiance to the government and the Communist Party. The Three-Self Movement was dedicated to the principles of self-government, self-support, and self-propagation—ironically the same principles by which many missionary organizations had been planning to organize the church in China, before "Liberation" in '49.

Gradually under the aegis of the Three-Self movement, independent Protestant churches of an evangelistic bent had been forced to close. Only those cooperating with the government could remain open. By the mid-fifties, some outstanding Christian church leaders and their congregations had come under severe pressure.

In the following decade, persecution of the church continued until it intensified during the

Cultural Revolution. From 1966 on, thousands of Christians not already in prison were brutally attacked and ridiculed. Those in detention were subjected to greater mental and physical pressures. Hundreds renounced the faith and betrayed other believers. No longer was there fellowship or trust; the scars of this terrible trial have remained with the purified Body to the present.

By the 1970s, the harsh repression of all openly Christian activities continued, although the fierce personal attacks, the mob trials, and physical torments at the height of the Cultural Revolution had ceased.

Other than word of extreme persecution, both physical and psychological, little had been heard of these believers for years. How could Hong Kong Chinese risk endangering these loved ones further by giving their names to total strangers? Especially when they could not be sure how the information would be used.

Joseph and Uncle Liu were touched by their love for the believers inside, and realized these Hong Kong Christians could not be expected to understand that they too shared that love. The two were further moved by the protectiveness extended to them also:

"You know that once you get inside, they may not let you leave the country again. You have the rest of your lives ahead of you. We see your love for the Lord. Why don't you let Him use you in some other work?"

These responses would be given over and over, as Joseph and Uncle Liu struggled with their three months of searching in Hong Kong.

Their first encouragement took place at a meeting held in a Bible school. During the gathering, Uncle Liu addressed the students and noticed an elderly lady sitting quietly among the young-looking group. After the meeting she introduced herself as Miss Woo and invited the pair home for coffee.

They gratefully accepted her invitation. After coffee and crackers, she said to Joseph, "I wonder if you and your uncle would pray for me? I am suffering from a hemorrhage and I know I will not have long to live unless God intervenes."

Although surprised by such a direct request, they immediately prayed for her, believing that she would be delivered from her illness. The next day, Miss Woo phoned Joseph.

"Praise God, I've been healed! As you prayed, I felt something happen inside and now I am completely well. Please, I want you to come and be my guests during your stay here in Hong Kong."

Soon the pair moved in with Miss Woo, who quickly became a mother to both of them. She wanted to encourage them with their ministry so much that she would not let them help her with even the smallest task.

"But, Miss Woo," Joseph would protest, clutching a broom and dustpan. "I'm still young and you are an old lady. I also want to help you."

He never got any farther than that. Miss Woo shooed him back in his room before he could utter another word.

Still not able to find an opening among the Christians in Hong Kong, the two spent hours talking and praying about the trip. How could God be in it? There was no contact yet and the three months were drawing to a close. They would soon be crossing the border with no one definite to see.

In his heart, Joseph was hoping the trip would fall through. He remembered only too clearly the first China trip he had taken with his uncle a year before. Then the two had known that they would stand out because at that time it was normal for only old overseas Chinese to go inside to visit relatives. So they were not surprised when their baggage was thoroughly searched. They had not taken Bibles with them, but still the checks were harrowing. If they even once stepped out of line, there was always the danger of arrest and detention.

They also remembered the difficult conditions of their one chance to witness to their relatives. The encounter had taken place in their far-from-private living quarters in a large house shared with many other families. Private conversation was impossible.

Not fluent in the same dialect as his relatives, Joseph communicated his faith to them by notes. Although Chinese is spoken in many different dialects throughout the country, the actual writing of each is the same.

Joseph wrote his testimony on a piece of paper and passed it to the others. Someone would reply with a question on paper, and then his answer would come the same way. The final one to read it would crumple the paper and throw it into the fire.

At that time, it was still illegal to propagate one's faith in China. Joseph and Uncle Liu knew only too well the dire outcome if the authorities discovered what was happening.

The two men could still recall the tension of that visit and would have been only too glad not to return to that environment again.

Besides their fears about China itself, there was another problem. *Me.*

They were not quite sure what to do with their foreign friend or *gwailo*. If they associated openly with an American, there'd be little chance of gaining the trust of the Hong Kong Christians.

China regarded America as its number one enemy at that time. Large slogans, displayed on the streets of the major cities, proclaimed their message of hate. "People of the world, unite and defeat the U.S. aggressors and all their running dogs!" was a popular one.

No wonder Joseph and his uncle were careful not to mention anything about an American to those around them. The two were not even completely certain about my motives for the work.

The three of us usually met late, often returning home in the early hours. Hoping that Miss Woo would be asleep by then, Joseph would tiptoe to his room, quietly shutting the door behind him. Almost inevitably came the sound he dreaded most . . . the soft padding of Miss Woo's feet approaching the door. Her knock followed. Then the questioning would begin. "Who is this American?" she would ask, her brown eyes peering into Joseph's tired ones. "You should tell me."

How could Joseph tell Miss Woo about me, a "U.S. aggressor," who wanted to start a China ministry? As I agonized before the Lord, His love for His Chinese children seemed to grow within me until I felt weighed down with all that they were going through.

I would pray and walk for hours in the humidity of the heavy tropical evening around the streets where I lived in Manila. "Father, I sure don't like what's happening to China under communism. I feel sick over the thousands in prison. And thousands more being tortured in labor camps, not to mention those who have been killed.

"But, Lord, You know my life too, and yet You love me despite the terrible things I've done to people. If You can love me, then I can look at the people of China the way You look at me. And I can love them too.

"Father, there are 800 million Chinese out there. I know You care, because You died for every one of them. Show us the way to reach them. Will You trust us with one contact—soon, Lord?"

Nevertheless, trusting Him for that contact was

a battle. I had placed Joseph and Liu in Hong Kong and they hadn't found one lead during all these weeks. I found myself wondering whether I was right to have put them through this. Didn't God intend for them to make this trip for the suffering church?

Somewhere, deep inside, I knew the answer was "yes." It was as though God was urging me to ignore circumstances and just believe Him for the vital contact who could put us in touch with the church in China. As before, the teaching of old Mr. Roy came to mind: "Are you going to walk by faith, son? Or by sight? You know which way St. Paul chose."

To our surprise, the answer to our prayers had its origin in a dream. One night, before having even left for Hong Kong, Joseph had seen a map in his dreams. It depicted two southern provinces of China: Guangdong (Kwantung) and Fujian (Fukien). When he awakened, he thought about his dream, but couldn't understand it at first. Why had he been shown a map? If anything, he might have expected to see the land itself—the blue mountains, the paddy fields speckled with peasants at work.

But later, he understood the message. God seemed to be telling him that they were to go to China—to two special areas, in fact: Fujian and Guangdong.

Then, several days before they were due to leave for China, Joseph and Uncle Liu attended a service in the Kowloon YMCA. Afterwards, an elder of the church introduced them to a believer who had just come from China, where he had undergone severe persecution himself.

From the first, the Christian responded warmly. "Why don't you come to my home for a prayer meeting?" At the believer's home, they spent over an hour in prayer for China. Suddenly, during their time together the believer told Joseph and his uncle, "When you go to China, I'll give you the names of three people in Fujian and they will help you. They are some of the Christian leaders of the province."

Joseph and Uncle Liu found themselves close to tears of joy. After six long months of searching, they had gotten a breakthrough. And they realized, as they turned to each other with a smile, this was one of the two provinces in Joseph's dream!

By the time Joseph got home, however, fear gripped him. He knew he should be happy about the contact, but he wasn't. Turning to his Bible, he read Revelation and Daniel. He thought to himself, *These are two books which deal with the end times and if they catch me or put me in jail, at least I will know God's Word.*

Joseph even contemplated writing his parents a last farewell letter assuring them of his gratitude for the way they had raised him and provided for him.

The days went by. Then, despite their fear, Joseph and Uncle Liu booked their tickets. They knew they had to go, for God had already shown them He was authorizing the trip.

Before they were due to leave for China, they attended a fellowship meeting at which they met another believer, Mrs. Ho, originally from Shanghai. Breaking through traditional Chinese reserve, she greeted them with the warmth normally given to close relatives.

Joseph was baffled. Although she had not known they were coming, it seemed she had been waiting for them. That's how excited she was to see them.

"Please come into my lounge and let's share the goodness of the Lord," she said with her eyes glowing. Mrs. Ho spoke Mandarin with a Shanghai accent, which made it hard for them to follow all her conversation. But they did understand that while she had been praying, God had shown her two men fitting their description.

"I had a vision that you would come and now you are here," she explained. "You have obviously been sent to me by God, and so I have someone I want you to meet."

Then she called to a friend in a nearby house. This friend gave the name and address of a believer Joseph and Uncle Liu could contact in another province of China. That province was the second one on the map in Joseph's dream: Guangdong.

I flew to Hong Kong to see the two on their way. We knew it would be unwise for us to be seen together at the railway station, so I said goodbye the night before. I left them with the best gift I could find: some verses from Isaiah 45 in which the Lord promises "to open doors . . . that gates may not be closed," to "go before you and level mountains," to "break in pieces the doors of bronze" and to "give you the treasures of darkness. . . ."

We had no idea what "treasures" they might find in the spiritual darkness of China, and no inkling of what mountains might have to be leveled. But God was with them. The way He'd brought about the contacts was confirmation of His leading.

Now, they simply had to grasp His hand and go forward, confident that the Lord would pave the way before them.

TEN

CHINA, LET ME LOVE YOU

"Coming home February 20 Stop Father has been wonderful to us Stop Joseph Lee Stop." The cable had reached me just twenty-four hours before.

What's happening inside? Are they all right? Can they be in any danger? I'd asked myself a thousand times. Joseph and Uncle Liu were being exposed to a hostile government from which there was no guarantee of return. I'd been looking forward to this cable for five long weeks now.

I'd also been wondering whether they had made contact with the believers inside. *How are the Christians coping with the pressures of the government? Do they need our help? Was there even a secret church left inside the People's Republic?* Each time a question arose, I would talk it out with the Lord. Many times a day, Julie and I would stop to pray for the dedicated pair.

Now that the day of their return had arrived, I could hardly stand still. They would be meeting me in my tiny, box-like hotel room in Hong Kong.

"Praise God, you're safe!" I said when the two finally stood in my doorway. Tears welled up in my eyes, as I flung my arms out to greet them with a giant bear hug.

But even as I greeted them, I could tell something wasn't quite right. "You're okay, aren't you?"

The two smiled, but I felt they were masking something. "We are fine, Brother David. We are just tired. We are glad to see you again," Uncle Liu reassured me.

"Well, come on, sit down! Let's talk. Where do we begin? There've been so many questions I've been dying to ask you guys. Where would you like to start?" I stopped as a look of uncertainty clouded their faces. Something was definitely wrong, but as ever, the two were scrupulously polite.

"We would like to know how you are too, Brother David. How is your wife? Your kids?"

Our conversation never went beyond superficial pleasantries. When they finally left, I pondered their subdued response. Maybe they *were* tired as Uncle Liu had said. And maybe more would be forthcoming next time, as they said. Or would it?

Over the following days, I realized that they felt uncomfortable about sharing the precious information they had gathered. I realized now that the pair were being every bit as protective towards the believers in China as the Hong Kong Christians had been toward their relatives. Could Joseph and Uncle Liu really trust all their information with an American?

"Lord, I've got an awful lot to learn about the Chinese. And I want to learn. The only way I can is for You to give me patience and understanding. Not only for these two, but for their people as well." With that prayer, I leaned back on the bed and closed my eyes. *China, let me love you,* I said silently.

Eventually, the Lord did answer my prayer. A little at a time, communication between us grew. Over the following weeks and months, the picture emerged.

I began to see a church which had been purified by fire, a church which had experienced the same pains Jesus had experienced. This church had come to understand Golgotha itself. I had never known that place.

"And can we stand with them?" I wanted to know. "Do they want our help?"

By way of answer, Joseph recounted a story he and Uncle Liu had been told by a pastor they had met in Xiamen (Amoy).

"In 1969, the Red Guards staged a typically violent rampage on the little group of believers. They confiscated the pastor's Bible, along with those of the entire congregation.

"The Bibles were taken out into the streets and burned in one huge bonfire. Then the pastor was put in prison again. He had been in prison for nine years before that. His brother has been in jail for fourteen years. Because of solitary confinement in a dark room for so long, he can no longer see. Because of the torture and malnutrition, he can no longer walk.

"His brother is still in prison. If he renounces Jesus as Lord and publicly declares that Chairman Mao is God, then he can come out.

"After the pastor's Bible was taken, he prayed, 'Lord, you know the communists have taken every possible copy of your Word. You have seen those copies burning. I ask you, would you please speak to someone *outside* of China? Would you cause them to prepare the Scriptures for our people. And Lord, would you bring those Bibles into our land?'

"Tears began to flow from the pastor's eyes when he told us that this day he had seen the answer to his prayer."

At that point in Joseph's story, I found it hard to choke back my own emotions. The three of us stopped to thank God for the faithfulness of His leading.

Joseph also shared the story of their visit with Pastor Henry Chai, their last contact in Fujian province. Though by this time they had no Bibles left to give, the middle-aged pastor still received them warmly.

"I'm so pleased you have come at this time, because our meeting is about to start," Pastor Chai said. Joseph and Uncle Liu sat down, surprised. Where was the "congregation" besides the pastor and his young daughter? An old clock ticked noisily as they waited politely.

After a short time, two people arrived and were introduced. A little later, someone else "drifted in" as if on a social visit. This pattern continued over twenty minutes until fifteen people had crowded into the small room.

The service was very different from those which Joseph and his uncle were used to in their home church. A few unaccompanied hymns were sung from memory, but very quietly. Then the pastor asked the two "visitors" to testify before the group.

The highlight for the congregation was the sharing of God's Word. Although Pastor Chai owned a copy of the Bible, he never brought it out for worship services. If an outsider were to surprise them, the Bible would immediately expose their activity. Instead, while the pastor was preparing the sermon for the week, he would carefully memorize the Scripture verses to quote during the service.

Joseph and Uncle Liu watched the congregation drink in the words. Later, the two learned that this was virtually the group's only contact with God's Word during the week. The pastor's sermon, urging them all to greater holiness in their living, was especially moving. Knowing what a price these believers must have already paid for their faith, both men felt very convicted by the message.

After the service, the congregation left at well-spaced intervals just as they had arrived. Uncle

Liu wondered whether the officials had ever been aware of Pastor Chai's activities. In response, the pastor told them what had happened to him during the Cultural Revolution, when persecution had been the most intense.

He had been subject to many kinds of suffering. On one occasion, he had been arrested at gunpoint and called upon to deny Christ. The Red Guards assured him that if he would simply deny Jesus, he would be freed. But he would not.

For several hours, they continued haranguing him, but he would not meet their demands. Eventually, they followed another ploy. They produced a large color picture of Chairman Mao and began chanting over and over, "Kneel down before our great and wise leader." When Chai refused to comply, they grabbed him roughly by the shoulders and tried forcing him to his knees. After that failed, they decided to "encourage" him by savagely beating his legs with sticks. The attack was so brutal that he collapsed on the floor.

At last, the soldiers seemed satisfied.

"Brothers," Pastor Chai said to Joseph and Uncle Liu, "Not only I, but also my daughter has suffered. Because of our faith, she will not be permitted to pass her exams at school. And since the authorities know we are Christians, they will not allow her into the university."

As he saw their surprise, the pastor explained, "It is the same for all of our friends. Each of their children has suffered academically for the faith. Could you help me get my daughter out of China?"

Joseph and Uncle Liu agreed to do everything they could to help. "What about you, Pastor? Would you like to leave China yourself?"

"I have already had the opportunity to go to Hong Kong, but I have no wish to." With a look of peace on his face, he concluded by telling them that his place was in China where he could serve the flock the Lord had given him.

Uncle Liu told us about a special Bible school in Guangzhou where young Christians are trained to teach the Bible.

"But how can they meet for classes?" I wanted to know.

"That is just it. They don't," Uncle Liu said. "Their system is very simple. The teachers go to the pupils, one at a time, and from house to house, as though on social calls. With each lesson, both teacher and pupil place their very freedom on the line."

"How bad is their need for Bibles?"

"Some of those we visited had no Bibles at all, since many were publicly burned in 1966. Others had just one or two for worship meetings and stored them in secret places in between. Many had divided up their Bible in separate parts, so that members of the congregation could each take home a portion to be returned the following meeting, almost like a little library.

"Every group, every Christian we met, wanted us to return with Bibles. Brother David, we have promised to do everything we can to fulfill their requests."

"Amen to that," I responded. "Have they any way of reproducing the Scriptures inside?"

"Only by hand," Joseph explained. "We met one group of young people who would get up two to three hours before work every morning just to copy the Scriptures. But it is slow work, Brother David. And it takes them a long time to get very far."

We talked late that night. I found myself more heavily burdened than ever to get Scriptures into China. I longed to take them myself if only I could get into the country.

"Well, Brother David, although you can't get a visa to go yet, we can do the next best thing for you," said Uncle Liu.

"What's that?"

"We have taken many photographs during our weeks away. You set a time one evening and we'll show you all of them."

A short time later, Joseph and Uncle Liu showed Shan Kumar and me slides from their trip to China. We were particularly struck by the uniformity of the people. It was hard to tell the men from the women since they wore no make-up, and both sported simple, short hair styles. Even more extraordinary was the fact that the masses all dressed in the same drab, ill-fitting, blue overalls.

But when we saw close-up shots, we saw just how different each person was. An old woman with a well-lined face sat quietly in the bamboo chair outside her tiny home. Children smiled happily as they watched the ducks in a Guangzhou (Canton) park. An old man with white stubble on his chin stared up at the camera lens with a look of bewilderment in his eyes. Middle-aged parents rode their bicycles home from work, the toll of their daily labor evident in their tired bodies.

Each one was an individual, living a life of his own. And each one needed the love of Jesus.

"We have not mentioned this before, but there are many believers in China who told us that they believe a revival is underway in that land," Joseph said, pausing for our reaction.

"You mean to say," Shan responded, almost protesting, "that in a country where it's hazardous to propagate one's faith, they are seriously contemplating revival? They can't even afford to open their mouths for the Lord without risking imprisonment!"

"I know. At first, we could not believe it possible either. But it's already begun."

Joseph explained that twelve months before their arrival in Fuzhou (Foochow), two old ladies had been sensing a revival coming. They began a prayer meeting, certain that God was going to work in their area.

Their answer came by way of a visit from a wide-eyed, deaf-mute girl who was demon possessed. As the two women tried to show her affection, she retreated in a corner of the room. The women knelt beside her and surrounded her with their arms as they prayed for her to be healed. Suddenly, the girl let out an unearthly shriek, despite her inability to speak. Then, she became calm. From that day on, she was able both to hear and to speak.

News of her healing spread throughout the area, and soon others came to their home with prayer requests. God met each need.

One night, 200 people had gathered in their small place for a thanksgiving service, when suddenly a knock was heard over their singing. An officer of the People's Liberation Army stood outside the door with two of his enlisted men.

"What's going on in here!" he demanded.

"We're just holding a prayer meeting,"one of the women explained.

"And who are you praying to?" he sneered.

"We're praying to God."

The soldier's tone was condescending. "Oh, who is your God and what is He doing?"

One of the old ladies spoke up. "Our God is the One who made the heavens and the earth. He is a God who cares for you and cares for us. He became like us to die in our place and He rose again from the grave."

He didn't interrupt her, so she continued.

"When He was on earth, Jesus did many wonderful miracles and touched people with His love and compassion. We are here because He has been doing the same wonderful miracles in our midst."

The officer's confidence was a little shaken. "What has He been doing?" he asked.

"You see that one over there?" she replied. "He was sick in his stomach and the Lord touched him. And that one over there? He didn't have enough food. And we prayed to the Lord and the Lord provided food for him. This man here, his leg had a huge sore on it, and we prayed for him and the Lord healed him."

Even so, the officer was not convinced. "Look at my nose," he mocked. "It's disfigured, isn't it? I've been told I've got cancer. What can your God do about that?" For all his skepticism, the old woman discerned a look of need in his eyes.

She opened the door wider and invited him to sit on a chair in their midst. As they began to pray, he lowered his rifle to the floor and bowed his head. When the prayer was finished, the three military men left the house, making no attempt to break up the meeting.

That night, the officer felt a strange sensation in the afflicted area. Upon awakening in the morning, he found he was completely healed. The man was so excited he returned to the house.

"Tell me more about this God! I want to know all about Him!" His tone was urgent.

The two explained that Jesus loved him and died in his place so he might be reconciled to God. They pointed out that Jesus was ready to forgive him.

"Do you believe?" they asked. "Will you accept Jesus and start life over?"

He nodded. "I want to give my life, to Him, to enlist in His ranks."

News of the officer's conversion spread like wildfire through the town. And the regular meeting grew from 200 to 500 members.

The officer was given a copy of the Scriptures

and as he began to share his newly found faith, the meetings increased all the more. By the time Joseph and Uncle Liu had arrived in town, 1200 people had gathered in one meeting in a large house in Fuzhou.

It was a pattern we were to see repeated over and over again in China: God using signs and wonders, as He had done in Bible days, to draw people to Himself.

The authorities' retaliation, however, was every bit as strong as the movement's growth. They investigated immediately and, before long, had identified the five leaders of the revival. The day before Joseph and Liu arrived, these men had been arrested and as an example for the rest of the people, been made to look like circus clowns before the town. Their heads had been shaven, their faces painted, and they had to wear little dunce hats. After that, they were paraded through the streets and then taken to prison. To our current knowledge, two of the five are incarcerated to this day.

By the time Joseph finished his story, we had no doubt that a revival was smoldering in China. This was not the picture of believers in dwindling numbers which we had expected to find under communism. Here was a church so sold out for Jesus that He was able to work through them in a way far more powerful than through many of us in the outside world.

"How can we help them?" I asked. "What do they want us to do?"

"Well, of course, they constantly requested Scriptures," Liu replied. "But more important than that, they asked us to pray.

"They long to know that their brothers and sisters are upholding them daily in the Free World. Their bold stand for Christ costs them everything. And the shame of it, Brother David, is that they are already in daily prayer for us in the outside world."

Shan and I looked up in surprise. "What are they praying for, Joseph?" Shan asked.

His reply silenced us.

"They are praying that we not become too comfortable in our affluence lest our witness become weakened. They pray that the power of materialism will not extinguish our fire for the Lord."

ELEVEN
THE REAL CHINA?

A few days later, Shan saw us off at Kai Tak International Airport, which juts out into the shimmering Hong Kong Bay, crowded with traditional junks and fishing trawlers. As Joseph Lee, Uncle Liu, and I fastened our seat belts, we welcomed the prospect of soaring over the South China Sea, and of flying back to our families in Manila.

We also anticipated that the outside world's concern for China would likewise gain momentum and lift off the ground. Joseph and Uncle Liu carried their burden for China heavily and carefully. They even prayed to discern those friends with whom they could share some of their trip.

Some responded with enthusiasm and encouraged them to return to China. But far more often, they heard the old familiar warnings: "Can you be sure you can trust an American?" "China is still too dangerous," and "It's okay to pray for China, but more than that is impossible." The most unsettling response of all was: "Joseph, you're so young. You have your whole life before you. Why waste it on that country? You could do so much good elsewhere."

Why indeed? Joseph, Uncle Liu, and I met to compare reactions. It was almost an instant replay of what they had heard in Hong Kong before their trip to China. After all our expectation, it seemed we were back at square one. Still, we could understand those reactions. Mao was very much at the helm. It looked ridiculous, humanly speaking, to be talking of China at a time when the country was thoroughly sealed behind the Great Wall.

And yet hadn't the Lord been consistently teaching us to walk, not by sight but by faith?

"Father, there has to be a way of bringing East and West together." I continued my talks with the Lord around the sloping streets of my home area.

"There just has to be some way for Your people in the outside world to support Your people in China. We are all members of one Body—Yours, Lord. And You call for all parts of the Body to work together."

I recalled a conversation which Brother Andrew and I had shared long before I came to this work full time.

"David," Brother Andrew had said, "we need to bring together every person and every group who has an interest in the kingdom of God in China. We must encourage one another to work behind the Bamboo Curtain. Just think, if denominations and missionary organizations combined their knowledge and insights in one conference, how much more could be achieved!

"David, we want to be a doormat for any who want to get God's Word into China. It doesn't matter which organizations take the ten million Bibles inside, as long as they walk in response to God's leading."

The name for the conference had come later. After discussing our plans with David Wang of Asian Outreach in Hong Kong, we'd found the appropriate name: "Love China." After all, if we didn't have love for the Chinese, we couldn't begin to serve them.

For me and my co-workers, Joseph and Uncle Liu, the conference seemed to be the next step the Lord had in store for us. All of us threw our energies into the mammoth task of organizing it.

In the meantime, letters began trickling out regularly from the Christian contacts Joseph and his uncle had made in China:

I know of your concern for me...thank you very much for the money you sent ... I will offer your love as a fragrant offering to the Lord. God will surely bless you. ...

Another:

Thank God that under His wonderful leading we now have a regular Christian gathering. The group is composed of male and female youth.

And another:

Even though Christians in the Mainland cannot go into the church to worship God, we can gather about ten persons to worship in the house and have fellowship and prayers. Please pray for us.

Such letters were a tremendous source of encouragement, renewing our sense of urgency to pray and to work all the harder.

Not only was support money getting inside China, but also Bibles, largely through the delivery system set up along the various borders. At that time, we'd just concluded a delivery of 50,000 Gospels of John via one of those routes. Already 5,000 New Testaments, deposited among contacts in Afghanistan, Burma, Laos, and the Himalayas, had also been carried across into China.

Often these went by donkey. The books were loaded inside potato sacks, 100 in each sack, and two sacks to a donkey. At other times, they were carried by foot couriers who transferred them from hand to hand until they reached the delivery point inside. For the Bibles that went through the Burma route, we learned that each Scripture had to be handled by thirty-six people from the time it left the Philippines until its final destination inside China.

One report of the work came to us from a man who had a regular part in the lonely treks through the Himalayas:

The Scriptures you gave me have been taken into the Southeast. They have crossed the borders into the Mainland. Here my brother gave them to another brother, and he to another. They were passed on and on until all were delivered into the hands of God's people.

The travel is very tiring, very difficult. Crossing the mountains does not take a few hours, but rather many days of continuous walking. We take shelter in the wilderness under the shadow of huge boulders. In the villages we take refuge among the dwellers. These people are very poor. For me, the mountains are very high, and very cold. . . .

The verse accompanying this report came from Isaiah 52:7: *How beautiful upon the mountains are the feet of him who brings good tidings, who publishes peace . . . who publishes salvation, who says . . . God reigns.*

During this time, a second courier, Ana-Marie Chung, volunteered to travel through China's front door: the Hong Kong border. An overseas Chinese girl with a great burden for her own people, Ana-Marie had reestablished contact with some of the Christians Joseph and Uncle Liu had met during their travels behind the Bamboo Curtain.

One contact she met was Pastor Chai who had suffered so much for his faith. She, like Joseph and his uncle earlier, was deeply moved by his continued preaching and counseling in the face of persecution.

Having already distributed the few Bibles she had brought into China, Ana-Marie gave him her own expensive Bible. In appreciation for her sacrificial gift, he gave his own humble gift, a beautiful rendition of "What a Friend We Have in Jesus," sung in his rich baritone.

Shortly after this warm meeting came a chilling shock. News of her activities in other towns had finally reached the police, chiefly through an informant. In the next town on her itinerary, the police caught up with her at her hotel.

"We would like to invite you for questioning," they said politely. She complied, knowing the Lord was with her and resistance was useless.

That first afternoon she experienced their mode of questioning. She later told us, "It was brainwashing. They kept on asking me the same questions over and over: 'What is your name?' 'What company do you represent?' 'Who is with you?' and 'With whom did you get in touch here?'" They questioned her for four hours at a time.

She was told she wouldn't be released that day, but would be in good hands nevertheless. At night, a woman officer would keep her company. Though permitted to join the officers for meals, Ana-Marie decided not to eat until they released her. "I'm just following an old Chinese custom," she told them. "I eat only with my friends, not my enemies."

"We're friends," they insisted.

"No! You do not trust me. You treat me like an enemy of your country. I'm a visitor. I have already cooperated; I gave you my answers. Even if you question me for one hundred more days, my answers will not change. No, I cannot eat with you."

Though the questioning went on for the next three days, Ana-Marie remained steadfast. At last they gave in. Noting from her passport that her visa was about to expire, they had to release her without having gained any information for all their efforts.

"You know, you should be working for the Communist Party. We need girls like you," they told her. Ana-Marie smiled and breathed a secret prayer. She knew the One they really needed.

The officers crowded around to see her off. "What will you tell your friends about our country? What do you think of China?"

"What do I think of *my* country? I love it. Jesus loves it too. . . ." She was on her way.

Her ordeal brought home to us the danger of the work. The "spiritual battle" was no theoretical term. It perfectly described the nature of the confrontation as we sought to take the sword of the Spirit into this land where Satan had established control.

Ana-Marie, Joseph, and Uncle Liu had all experienced China from the perspective of ethnic Chinese visiting relatives. It was not until we heard of a *gwailo* or "foreign devil" who managed to take a trip that we began to see the other side of the coin: the tourist's China.

Todd Martin from FEBC had managed to take a trip in 1973 as a member of a "special interest group" under official invitation from the Chinese government. He had been booked on a highly restricted tour to visit Guangzhou, Beijing, and Shanghai.

The first thing that struck him was the almost "missionary zeal" of the communist tour guides. Moment after moment, they tried to impress the visitors with the progress the country had made under communism. Factories, schools, communes, anything at all to illustrate the government's achievements were shown.

Before visiting any new place, the tourists were

given an "orientation" session during which various members of the Revolutionary Committee bombarded them with facts and statistics for a half-hour or longer. To complete the persuasion process, cigarettes, cookies, candies, peanuts, tea, beer, and China's famous "Pearl River Orange" soft drink were provided.

Todd found the situation uncomfortable. The guides allowed them little freedom of movement. One morning in Shanghai, he got up at 5:30 A.M. to take photos of the people going through their slow-motion shadow boxing exercises on the banks of the Huang Pu (Hwang Pu) River. As he bent over to change film, a large crowd gathered.

When Todd returned for breakfast at 7:30, one of his guides greeted him. "Good morning, sir. Did you enjoy watching the shadow boxers this morning?"

"Indeed," replied Todd, "but how did you know I was up to see them?"

The guide smiled. "I saw you there, sir. . . ."

Todd and a couple of other Christians on the tour were anxious to discover if the Church had survived at all under Mao's regime. No photographs of churches had yet appeared in the Western press. They even questioned whether the church buildings were still standing.

Their background reading had told them of Mao's gradual closedown of all churches since his take-over in 1949. Reports varied but most seemed to concur that before "Liberation" just under two million baptized members were in the Protestant churches in China. Over 6,000 Protestant missionaries had also been working in the country.

After setting up its Three-Self Patriotic Movement in 1951, the government had spent the subsequent years closing more and more churches until only a fraction of the original remained. By the time of the Cultural Revolution in 1966, very few churches were still open for worship. Under the fanatical fervor of the Red Guards, the handful left were quickly shut down and often subjected to senseless destruction and violence.

It was not only the Christians who had suffered. The Red Guards attacked anything and everything they associated with the "bourgeois practices" of Imperialism. All apparent evidence of any religion was obliterated in China.

The worst excesses of the Cultural Revolution had come to an end by 1970, so that now, three years later, Todd and the other Christians on the tour wondered if there were any public sign of Christianity re-emerging. They knew of just one officially registered church. It was in Beijing and had been opened in 1972 to serve mainly the foreign diplomatic community there.

The other Christian tourists were the first to go hunting for churches in Guangzhou. During the bus tour they had glimpsed a church relatively near the hotel. Choosing a moment when the lobby was particularly busy, they slipped away through a side door. At the church, one of them stood in front of its bricked-up front door, while another crossed the street to get a photograph. He lifted his camera, focused, and was about to press the button when someone from the crowd nearby jostled him. As a result, the shot was blurred. The "saboteur" gestured to indicate he should not take any pictures of the church.

A moment later, a big black car pulled up beside the tourist standing in front of the church. A backseat window was rolled down, and a man spoke to him politely in English: "Would you like to take a ride?" The tourist replied just as courteously: "No, thank you. My friend and I were just out for a stroll." The man in the back seat persisted but the *gwailo* matched his persistence until eventually the car drove away.

"After all our reading," Todd told me, "this incident really gave us the creeps. The atmosphere was so tense you could have almost cut it with a knife."

Later they tried again to photograph a church in Beijing but again without success. Finally in Guangzhou, Todd managed to get the photo he wanted.

He had glimpsed the twin spires of the Catholic cathedral on one of their tours and set out early one morning to find it. On his way he became lost and found himself wandering through the little back streets of the city.

The cleanliness of the area struck him. Although the homes were very old and often in need of repair, they were nonetheless scrupulously tidy, just like those on the prescribed tourist trail. Todd realized it was not simply a cosmetic clean-up for the tourists.

By now Todd was well "off limits" and still no closer to finding the cathedral. Suddenly he spied a small church right in the middle of the block. On the other side of the street, a man was busy cutting wood. Todd approached him and made a big fuss about taking the laborer's picture as he stacked his pile of timber.

"Of course," Todd later explained, "I focused on the church behind him. To have actually found one I could photograph was like finding gold!"

Later, back at the hotel, a fellow tourist approached him. "You were lucky to get your photograph this morning," he said.

"Why?"

"Well, I was walking some distance behind you, and when I got there I tried taking a picture of the old man cutting wood, but someone came out of the shop behind me, tapped me on the shoulder, and told me I was not allowed to take the photograph."

It had become obvious to the tourists that the pressure being exerted in China was coming not merely from the party officials and cadres. The people themselves were now so committed to the "cause" that they had become each other's keeper.

No matter where they went, the group never escaped some expression of the government's "gospel." Slogans on the streets, posters on the walls, giant pictures of Mao Zedong, all declared basically the same belief in the New China. P.A. systems also blasted forth the propaganda. It was perhaps to be expected that one should find loudspeakers proclaiming the virtues of the regime in Beijing's Tian An Men Square. But the same thing was repeated along the streets of Beijing, Shanghai, and Guangzhou—everywhere the tourists traveled.

So persuasive was the message that the tourists came away feeling that they had visited a land flowing with milk and honey.

"Their response was past the point of reason," said Todd. "I suppose, to start with, we were dealing with mythology's Middle Kingdom, the Great Cathay. That, coupled with the Party's excellent salesmanship, made most of the tourist party quite euphoric about the country."

I recalled what Brother Andrew had said about communism being a religion. It seemed more evident than ever that Mao had set out to win not only the people's minds, but their hearts and souls as well.

With the report files of Joseph, Liu, Ana-Marie, and Todd open before me, I sensed the full force of the communist juggernaut we faced. Its power was blatantly manifest, but also terrifyingly subtle. The Great Wall was a reality. I wondered how on earth we were ever going to penetrate it. How could we bring any significant aid to our brethren inside?

What chance did we have? We were a handful of people incapable both of outwitting communist propaganda, and of diminishing its awesome strength.

The close-up shots from the slides Joseph and Uncle Liu had shown us again flashed into my mind. "I love these people, Lord," I whispered, "and if I do, how much more *You* must love them. You died for every one of them."

And they don't even know it, I thought. *They may never have the chance to hear of Jesus as they spend their lives captive to the communist ideology.*

The impossibility of the task overwhelmed me. *Hey, but wait a minute, that's not right. Who has the ultimate control over even the communist regime?* The words of the Great Commission rushed back to me: *"All authority in heaven and on earth has been given to me."* Final authority had been given to *Jesus*, not to even the most powerful of human governments.

The rest of Jesus' words came back with familiarity: *Go therefore and make disciples of all nations. . . .* No matter how fearsome a government might look, we were still to *go.*

"Yes, Sir!" I said to the Lord. Then I stood up and asked Beng to call the local travel service. There was work to do!

TWELVE
HARD KNOCKS AND OPEN DOORS

For months now I had tried every available path to get into China. The travel service was one. As always, my secretary, Beng, returned with the same reply: "They are very sorry, David. They still can't organize a trip for you. Perhaps if you would call in a few weeks. . . ."

It was the same response I'd gotten on my numerous "pilgrimages" to the China Travel Service in Hong Kong. Every time I went to the Crown Colony I would try both offices: the one in Kowloon and the main one on the Island.

"We are sorry, but at this time it is impossible for you to visit China," a polite but unsmiling counter clerk always told me. "We will take your name and address, and contact you if there is any change in the situation."

The call never came, but I would return on my next visit to Hong Kong. My brawny frame and pleading look became well known to the staff. Sometimes I would take my wife, Julie, and our three children along to chat with the officials. Always upon entering the office, I would give a silent prayer that the Chinese staff would see beyond me and my persistence to the deep love of Jesus Himself.

As I clocked up my thirtieth visit, I detected a slight thaw. The manager called me, "Now, sir, why do you keep coming back? Why do you want to go to China?" I could imagine his real thoughts. *Can't I get through this thick head? If I've told him once, I've told him thirty times. And he still keeps coming back!*

But the Lord had been teaching me patience and instructing me more and more about loving China.

"I am your friend," I replied with a smile. He knew I meant it. What he didn't know about were the hours I'd spent pleading China's case before the Lord.

While the travel service had been consistently refusing me, I had tried other possible channels. Whenever I went to a country which had diplomatic relations with China, I would try to visit their embassy in an attempt to get my longed-for visa. All to no avail. I was getting nowhere fast.

However, although unable to enter China itself, I still found myself traveling frequently. Too frequently, I thought at times. It was becoming increasingly harder to leave my family so often. Each goodbye became more difficult than the one before. Yet the family continued giving me the support which helped keep me going.

On one occasion, while passing through Hong Kong on my way to our annual conference in Holland with Brother Andrew, I got a call from Julie.

"It's Dawn, honey. She had an accident at school today." Julie was obviously trying to hold back tears. "She's broken both her arms."

"She's what?"

Julie described the full details of the accident. Both of Dawn's arms were in plaster casts. By the time Julie had finished, I was ready to catch the next plane home.

"You don't have to do that. That's not why I rang." Julie was emphatic.

"I can't let you go through something like this on your own!"

"But we're not on our own. The Lord's with us. Honey, I just felt I had to let you know so you could be praying for us."

"I'll come home," I insisted. "It's not fair to you."

"Dave, the kids and I believe you ought to go. The Lord has important work waiting for you. We all want you to go."

I'd never put the phone down more reluctantly. My family had been contending with so much lately.

Just a couple of months before, when I was once again visiting the borders, our family car had broken down while Julie was driving along a busy highway. She had had no option but to leave it there and return home to the family. Upon returning the next morning, she found an empty shell. Thieves had removed the wheels, battery, and even parts of the engine.

This ministry was costing them, no doubt about it. Yet Julie's words of commitment to the task echoed in my mind as I set out for Holland: "The Lord's with us. . . . We all want you to go."

The meeting in Holland, held October 1974, turned out to be a milestone for Brother Andrew's work. Gathered in his hometown were his own team from Europe, the North American team, and teams from the African and Asian regions.

Although each group was in regular contact with the others, there was, as yet, no official organizational link-up among the various parts. Brother Andrew, always wanting things kept small, had deliberately shied away from a large-scale organization.

That year, however, we realized that the time had come to establish one body with branches wherever the Church was being persecuted. With

Africa, Asia, Europe, and the States represented, it now remained for us to form bases in the Middle East and Latin America.

The name of the organization, "Open Doors with Brother Andrew," had come as an earlier outgrowth of Brother Andrew's idea. He'd told us, "We should never say that any country is closed to the gospel of Jesus Christ. Jesus told us to go into *all* the world, and if we are obedient to His command, He can open the door of any country for us. Revelation tells us, 'I have set before you an open door, which no man can shut.'"

Open doors. Hadn't God promised them in His Word? But where was my own open door to China? A few weeks later, back in the Philippines, I had an unexpected visit from a man who seemed positive he had found a way into the People's Republic. He was Harold Whitman, a travel agent from Great Britain, who had deliberately made a stopover in Manila to contact me.

"Brother Andrew suggested you might be interested in knowing that I'm going to China without a visa."

"Without a visa?" *The man can't be serious!* I thought. "That's impossible!"

"All things are possible," he replied. "After this place, I fly to Hong Kong. From there, I go to Seoul, from Seoul to Tokyo, Tokyo to Beijing, from there to Hanoi, then on to Bangkok, and finally back to London."

Either this guy is a nut or else he has plenty to teach me about getting to China by faith. I needed to know more. "How did all of this start?" I finally asked.

"Well, I took my leading from a verse in Matthew chapter 7: 'Ask, and it will be given you; seek and you will find; knock and it shall be opened.'"

"Okay, Harold, who'd you ask?"

"I asked the authorities in China if I could visit

them, and they said 'yes.' They telexed me: 'We have a room waiting for you in Beijing. You'll be welcomed on your arrival.'"

But without a visa? How could it be possible? I thought.

"Since I'm a travel agent, I naturally turned to the guide books around me. I've discovered you can fly in from Tokyo to Beijing and from there to Hanoi. What's more, if you want to get from Beijing to Hanoi, you have the 'inconvenience' of staying seven whole days in Beijing."

Seven days! I'd have given a lot for even one or two.

"When I get to Tokyo, I just get on the plane and they take me to China."

"But the visa?"

"Oh, they'll give me one when I get there."

"Man, if it works for you, send me a postcard from Beijing because I want to know!" I wanted to believe what he said, but after all my attempts, was *his* way really that easy?

Three weeks later a postcard arrived from China. It was from Harold. So it *had* been easy. All I'd needed was a jolt to my system.

I lost no time after that. A friend named Derek, Shan Kumar, and I followed Harold's example and soon got an official invitation to Beijing.

The three of us traveled to Tokyo to await our flight to Beijing, China's "forbidden city." On the day of our departure, all seemed to go smoothly. Our passports passed inspection at the counter of China's own airlines, CAAC. The Chinese clerk checked the computer to confirm our flight. He tore off the coupons on our tickets, gave us our boarding passes, and took our baggage. As I stood watching the three pieces of luggage on the conveyor belt, I thanked God we were finally on our way.

And then it happened. Almost involuntarily,

Derek found himself voicing his inner thoughts. "It's too easy," he murmured, shaking his head. The man behind the counter looked up, startled.

"What's too easy?"

"It's just that we don't have our visas for China," Derek said, trying to appear nonchalant.

"Oo-ooh," said the man with a wealth of meaning.

We were suddenly involved in a complicated exchange with the clerk, who ordered us to return our boarding passes and follow him upstairs to talk.

"You can't go. You don't have a visa in your passports. As you said, 'It was too *easy*. . . .'"

We explained that our flight had been confirmed and our hotel rooms specified, but he wouldn't listen.

I stood on the ramp while we waited for our bags to return. I felt completely dumbfounded. Nearby was our plane, a CAAC Boeing 707 painted white with a bright red Chinese flag and five golden stars on its tail. As it taxied down the runway, part of me went with it.

If only that counter clerk had not taken offense, we would have been on that plane. Why had he taken an idle comment and thrown it right back into our faces?

That day, I learned another lesson. When God is putting something together, it always fits. In that sense, it's "easy." We just had to trust Him and go forward with confidence and faith. In this battle, "walls have ears," and Satan can use a moment's hesitancy to thwart us. We couldn't afford to entertain any doubts. We were simply to follow and allow God to make it as "easy" as *He* wanted to.

Meanwhile, the date for the weeklong "Love China" conference was steadily approaching.

Shan was program director of the activities, but between us, we had to come up with a theme and publicity material for the conference. After much prayer and thought, Shan suggested the prayer theme: "Lord Jesus, through us let the people feel Your love."

Several weeks later, delegates filing into the conference room in one of Manila's big hotels saw two sights: a wall-length, blown-up photograph of communist soldiers on the march and the words of the prayer in large letters.

"Love China '75" was the first full-scale gathering since 1949 of evangelicals concerned about the Christian witness in China. More than 430 delegates from twenty-three countries gathered to consider the best way to give the Chinese people the gospel of Jesus Christ.

After the conference William Willis, one of the main speakers, and his wife Fanny flew to Hong Kong with Julie and me. We had first met them during the Ralph Bell Crusade held while we were on furlough in the States. At that time I had shared my vision for China with this Welshman. He, in return, had committed himself to praying daily for me. I knew that saintly old man devoted seven hours to prayer every day. His fervor for the Lord, coupled with his shock of white hair and his authoritative manner, reminded me of an Old Testament prophet.

Now during the "Love China" conference, we had resumed our friendship and would be traveling together.

When we got to Hong Kong, he spent the first day there in prayer. During lunch the following day he finally joined the rest of our group. After the meal, he took me aside. "Young man," he said, "the Lord has given me a message for you. But I'm not to tell you until I've looked into China."

"Can't you tell me now?" I asked, feeling a bit

impatient. But Mr. Willis was firm, and I didn't argue.

The following day, we took our wives to the Lok Ma Chao Look-out, the famous tourist spot in the New Territories from which one can see directly into China itself. It seemed we could almost touch the people separated from us by only the narrow, winding Shum Chun River.

Soon after, Mr. Willis told me what the Lord wanted me to know. "The door into China will open and never be closed for you and your friends. You will be able to go in and out as you please." He paused, allowing those words to sink in. "Can you believe that, young man?"

"I believe it." And I meant it.

Gazing into the distant blue-green hills of China, I thought, *Lord, you know I'm prepared to believe it. But how is it possible? How, Lord?*

A few weeks later, I again made application to visit the People's Republic, this time with my whole family. At last, we were told by Hong Kong's China Travel Service that it *might* be possible to get visas. In fact, it looked as though our visas were being processed. Then, unexpectedly, the Russian Embassy in Beijing was bombed. The word from the China Travel Service was crushing: "No more visas can be issued until the trouble is dealt with."

My family coped well with the news. "Guess the Lord has other plans for us," said Dawn. Our three D's had grown to trust God more and more in recent months, especially as they had seen Him continuing to meet our personal needs.

While in prayer one day, I'd asked the Lord about a car for me to use for the work. The constant use of public transport had been eating up funds, and I felt certain a car would be more economical.

"Why don't we have one, Lord?" I asked Him.

In the quiet of the moment, His voice seemed to answer: *Because you never asked me. I would have given you a car by now if you had turned to me.*

Later in the day, my children and I visited an auto dealer and were drawn to a brand-new green Toyota.

"That's a knock-out, Dad!" David said.

"Tell you what, why don't the three of us pray over this car and ask Jesus if He would find a way to let us own it for the work?" I asked.

They nodded. Together we placed our hands on the car and prayed, asking the Lord to allow us to have it. "And, Lord?" I asked. "We are thanking you in advance for it."

The next day, I returned to the car lot. Although he knew I had no money, the car dealer suggested I take it right away and pay for it in thirty days.

"We trust you for the money and believe in the work you're doing," he said. I was a total stranger! But with a grateful heart, I drove the car home to a very amazed family.

The money didn't come in thirty days. It came in twenty! Prayerful friends in Rolling Hills, California, once again unaware of our needs, had sent funds to help cover our family expenses.

So, if ever our kids had experienced answered prayer, it was that time. As a family, we now had to trust Him with our visit to China as well.

Since the China trip was to be followed by a trip to Holland, we decided to take a vacation retracing St. Paul's journey to the seven churches. This would be our first furlough in six years. It was also my way of saying "thank you" to my family for their patience and support of the ministry.

During our sightseeing, I had the clear sense that God was telling me to go to Rumania. It was the same kind of inner prompting I had had about the green Toyota. "Why, Lord?" I asked. In response, it seemed that God was telling me my answer would come from Brother Andrew in Holland.

"Of course, David!" Brother Andrew's face lit up. "Of all the countries in Eastern Europe, only Rumania and Albania are allies of China. The rest are linked with the Soviet Union. If you go to Rumania, you'll have no problem getting into China. Do you know you can even fly from Bucharest to Beijing? The Spirit of the Lord is talking to you.

"I say go, David. Take your family to the United States and then come back here to Holland from California. We'll arrange a trip for you to Bucharest.

"And, since you're going there," he said with an infectious smile, "why not take along some Bibles for the Rumanian Christians?"

Although Andrew and I met together for serious work, we also managed to relax with our families. They also felt the same bond which the two of us experienced. During our recreation we took outings together, enjoying Holland with its charming canals and windmills. My family especially appreciated the cool air which was such a contrast to the constant humidity of Manila.

Before we left, Brother Andrew and his wife Cory presented each of our kids with a pair of authentic Dutch wooden clogs. With typical thoughtfulness, they had chosen ones with an American color scheme of red, white, and blue. They knew the three D's loved their homeland. Besides, it was 1976, America's 200th birthday!

I followed Brother Andrew's counsel. For the final leg of our furlough, my family and I spent three weeks visiting family and friends in California, and celebrating America's Bicentennial.

After seeing Julie and the children off on a plane for Manila, I returned to Holland. Awaiting my arrival were a ticket to Bucharest and large bundles of Bibles.

On the morning of my flight, Hans, Brother Andrew's assistant, took me to the airport. As we drove past colorful fields of tulips damp from the night's rain, we suddenly saw two magnificent rainbows arched across the sky.

"Why, look!" Hans said. "Today you'll enter two communist countries. The rainbows are your confirmation of peace that you won't meet any storms in Czechoslovakia and Rumania."

"But there should be *three* rainbows. I'm going to Beijing, too," I countered.

"Well, two out of three isn't bad."

Then a half hour later, I saw it—the third rainbow in the sky. "That means I'm going to get into China," I exclaimed delightedly, settling back in my seat to enjoy the trip.

Those three rainbows proved to be confirmation indeed. In Rumania, the Lord opened doors for His Word as ninety Scriptures found their way unhindered into the hands of the believers. Now it remained for the door to open into the People's Republic.

But when our plane en route to China touched down in Karachi, Pakistan, the door seemed to be shutting right in my face. And it was a body blow, quite literally, that floored me. For two-and-a-half days I lay writhing in pain from one of Karachi's notorious viruses. My stomach was in knots. I had a fever which left me completely exhausted.

As I lay on the bed, doubts crowded my mind: *David, forget the Beijing deal. They won't give you the promised visa. Besides you're sick. Man, you've been mistaking your own will for His. See, He's sent this illness to show you that you're wrong. Wrong!*

The room seemed to spin around. I felt furnace heat in my head. Even the free-flowing perspiration couldn't put it out. And then all of a sudden I realized that God *did* want me to go to China. How else could I explain that unexpected leading to come via Rumania? This then had to be the work of the "enemy." I knew I was in a spiritual battle and I should be fighting, not surrendering to the enemy's plans.

On my knees, I prayed, "Lord, you've already defeated Satan on the Cross. Not in my own strength, but in Yours I claim the victory." Within a couple of hours my fever left me, the cramps completely stopped, and I felt as if I'd never been ill at all.

That evening my step was light as I walked into the waiting jet. The midnight flight over the Himalayas was unforgettable. Looking down, I saw the spectacular mountains with their jagged snowcapped peaks, fluorescent in the moonlight. Our Boeing 707 was winging its bumpy way eastward.

At six o'clock the next morning, I realized that for the first time I was looking at the People's Republic of China from the air. Pressing my face against the window, I gazed on the towns and villages and long stretches of cultivated land. Down in those green and brown patches lived the people for whom I had prayed, worked, and lived since 1972. Now I felt truly one with them. In a sense, I was coming home.

THIRTEEN
ONE STEP AHEAD

When we taxied to a stop, green-uniformed soldiers immediately surrounded us and began filtering onto our plane. A customs officer addressed us at the front. "Ladies and gentlemen," he said in perfect English. "Please present your passports."

As he began collecting them, I thought, *Oh, Lord, my passport doesn't even have a visa in it. Now what's going to happen?"* When he reached me, he said politely, "We've been waiting for you, sir. Please follow me."

He took me to the immigration department where he began processing my application for a visa. When the paper work was completed, he disappeared. Ten minutes later, he returned with my papers. Handing me my passport, now stamped with the official visa stamp, he said, "Welcome to the People's Republic of China."

I gratefully recalled the often repeated words of Brother Andrew: "Since Jesus has already given us instruction 'to go' on *His* authority, we don't need to wait for any further permission. Once we step out, God will do the rest." Now I had seen the truth of it with my own eyes!

"But sir," the immigration officer then said, "you can only stay for a few hours. A major earthquake has occurred here and everyone has been moved into the streets."

That famous earthquake of 1976 had caused death and destruction almost without precedent in recorded history. I later learned that as many as 750,000 were estimated to have died in the catastrophe. The city of Tianjin had been hit the worst, but shock waves had also reached the capital of Beijing.

The people and their tragedy struck me deeply. I saw privileged members of the Communist Party in their gray uniforms and peasants with faded, threadbare clothes and drawn, sallow faces etched with hopelessness. Others perhaps had come from the cities since their faces were smoother and more filled out.

Many cried openly. I realized that despite ideological differences, they were behaving like any other group of people after a tragedy of this magnitude.

Now you've seen them, David, the Lord seemed to be telling me. *These are the people I've laid on your heart. I wanted you to see them in a moment of great tragedy when they were most human, most vulnerable, most lovable—when no communist ideology and nothing on earth, except My own comforting, could ease their pain.* Thus, while disappointed by having to leave so soon, I understood why the Lord had allowed me to visit at this time.

When my plane touched down at Manila Airport, Julie was waiting for me. On the way home she said, "You remember your formal request for an invitation to visit the People's Republic?" I nodded, clearly recalling the letter I'd sent to Beijing several months earlier.

"Well," she said, with a twinkle in her eyes, "you have an answer here. It just happens to be. . . ." Her voice trailed off as if to keep me in suspense. ". . . an official invitation from the government for you to visit as soon as it's convenient."

I could hardly believe the good news! Here I'd

just returned from China and soon I'd be on my way back. The immigration official had said I'd be welcomed anytime. William Willis had said the same thing. The Lord had opened the door for me and no one would be able to shut it.

Ninety days after getting the formal invitation from China, I was on my way back. This time I went with James Wee, Billy Wee's younger brother. We took the train to China from Kowloon station in Hong Kong to the border post of Lo Wu.

When the train came to a halt, James and I prayed silently, for this was where our bags would be searched. We'd decided James should bring only his personal Bible, while I'd take along twenty Chinese Bibles for delivery to Tan Hoc Tue, one of Joseph's contacts in Guangdong Province.

Then came the moment we'd been waiting for. The customs official motioned us into the search area where he asked James to open his bags. James showed him his camera, jewelry, currency, and cassette recorder. The man seemed content enough until he noticed the large black Bible.

"What's this?" he asked, thumbing through it with interest.

"I'm a Christian," James said with a friendly smile. "That's my personal Bible."

The impassive officer told James he could take his Bible through since it was in English. Imagining what his response might be if he saw the twenty Chinese Bibles I had, I prayed all the harder.

I was next. Trying to appear casual, I moved my case and shoulder bag along the bench toward the officer and prepared for the confrontation.

"That's okay, sir," the man said, waving me on.

"I beg your pardon?" I asked in disbelief.

"You can move on, sir. No need to check. . . ."

That's all I needed to hear! I wasn't about to

hang around for him to change his mind. With a thankful heart, I retrieved my luggage and followed James.

After a sumptuous lunch provided by the Chinese government, we took a two-hour train ride to Guangzhou.

As the train made its way through the countryside, we saw peasants hard at work in the rice paddies. Bent double, some were planting seedlings, while others wielded heavy wooden farm implements. The fields themselves were in various stages of the rice cycle: newly planted patches awash with brown muddy water; young plants in clusters of dark green; and mature areas of bright yellow-green in sunlight.

On the edge of the neat paddy fields, groups of buildings nestled close together, in quiet tones of ochre, cream, and brown. It seemed these had stood for many years at the mercy of wind and rain. Paint was peeling. Walls were crumbling. The tiled roofs were breaking away at the corners. Yet the subtle colors of the buildings, set against the various shades of the fields and mountains, gave the scene a beauty all its own. There was a charm which made us feel transported from one world into another.

When we finally arrived in Guangzhou, it was October 23, 1976, the day Hua had been proclaimed Chairman in place of Mao. The entire city was alive with celebration. A cacophony of firecrackers surrounded us all the way to our hotel. After checking in our bags, we returned to the street. By that time, an impressive procession had gotten underway.

At first, I thought only the green-clad soldiers had been called out to pay homage to the new leader. Suddenly, the sea of marchers seemed to bear down upon James and me. Then, I realized there were just as many people in blue as in green.

These were Chinese civilians who had spontaneously joined the throng, bright with expectation of a better future under Hua. All seemed to be looking heavenward in an almost religious display of nationalistic fervor.

But what of the ultimate future? I thought. *Lord, how many of these people will have a chance to hear of you before they've burned out their lives working for Mao, Hua, whoever? Each will spend his life giving his all for the State. But upon his death, what will he have gotten from the State in return?*

That evening, as we walked through Guangzhou we glimpsed the double-edged significance of Hua's accession to power.

Stepping from our hotel, we felt the hot, sauna-like air clutching at us. I was wearing a blue denim outfit complete with a Mao cap, in an attempt to identify with the people. At the end of our street was a crowd of about 3,000 standing near an enormous billboard. As the only Westerners in that group, we got many long, hard looks. We smiled, but most glanced away, embarrassed to have made eye contact.

We watched while a poster of the newly denounced "Gang of Four" was being pasted into position. Madam Jiang (Chiang), Mao's widow, and three radicals, Yao Wen Yuan, Wang Hongwen, and Jiang Qing, formerly from the Politburo, were depicted in ridiculous poses. They looked like pigs skewered on a barbecue. Mao's discredited wife wore a black evening gown and had rings on her fingers and bells on her toes. She also had a ring through her nose, while tusks hung from her nostrils. The picture exuded decadence and a ferocious, animal-like appetite for power. Within the week, the entire world would hear about the "Gang of Four."

Brother Andrew had told me at our very first

meeting, "If they do not have an enemy on the outside, they create one on the inside. That's why there are never-ending purges in communism." It was all consistent with the pattern of China's "religion."

My thoughts were suddenly interrupted by three soldiers with rifles bearing down on the crowd. Since James and I were the only foreigners, they stared at us with particular interest. Then, since the group's gathering was a peaceful one, the soldiers went away.

Quickly making our way back to the hotel, we wound through the alleyways. In passing, we saw narrow, crumbling brick houses unevenly leaning against each other. Clothes, drying on wires across the alleys, fluttered like flags signalling that life existed on the inside. The muted light from low-watt bulbs, the old banyan trees lining the road, and the yellow moon slung low across the trees gave the scene an air of timelessness.

For James, however, the present was very real. Back at the hotel he was subdued, and understandably so. Poor James feared the prospect of a Bible delivery in light of the strident militancy we'd witnessed during the day.

He knew the penalty for any wrong move could easily be arrest and detention. He might never see his family again. "Let's pray, Brother David," he asked me. Still, despite our praying, he spent a restless night. The following two nights were no better.

On the fourth day, however, we traveled to the town where Mr. Tan lived. I stayed alone to pray, while James went to his house. My Western looks would have drawn too much attention. James brought him personal gifts of food and clothing, but arranged to deliver the Bibles the next day.

In the evening, James' feelings of uneasiness

were stronger than they had been even earlier in the week. Both of us fasted and prayed around the clock until 11:30 the following morning, yet James still felt the same way.

It seemed that God was indeed cautioning us. "Don't take the Bibles," I told James. "Just meet with Brother Tan anyway. I'll stay behind to pray some more."

When James got to the meeting place, a restaurant, he looked around for Brother Tan, but there was no sign of him. Approaching the taxi which had driven him there, he stopped in his tracks. Police were combing every cubic inch of the cab.

James did the most natural thing; he quietly returned to the restaurant and ordered a meal.

"My chopsticks were shaking, Brother David," he later told me with a weak smile. By the time he returned to the taxi, the police were gone.

How thankful we were that James had taken no Bibles. Later when Brother Tan told us he *had* been in the restaurant, but God had not allowed them to meet, we were doubly thankful. God had been one step ahead of us all the way!

Although the Bibles were still safe in my suitcase, we were not downhearted when we left the next day. We'd seen God at work in our eight days there. He had given us the chance to look into the very face of communism, as well as to make contact with believers.

He had also protected us at every turn. If the Bibles had been found even at customs, all our future deliveries would've been jeopardized! Above all, the Lord had taught us the essential lesson of walking in response to His leading only. That lesson would prove fundamental to all future courier work.

We felt disappointed, of course, that we'd been

unable to deliver the Scriptures, but God in His perfect timing had had other plans.

And after all, we were there to do *His* will, not ours.

After our time behind the Bamboo Curtain, I was more determined than ever to support the believers inside. By now my old friend Robert Foster had joined us fulltime, and all of us in Manila were concentrating our energies on providing Bibles and financial aid for the contacts Joseph had made.

Early in 1977 James and I had planned another trip into China, this time with our wives and Brother Andrew. We would deliver Scriptures to a contact in Guangdong, and while there, James had planned to visit his friend, Tan Hoc Tue, to make the promised Bible delivery.

On his earlier trip inside, James had had no trouble obtaining his visa, but not this time. As he prayed about the situation, he felt the same hand of restraint which he had experienced in Guangzhou. For some reason the Lord was telling him not to go on the trip. So, finally on the day of our departure, we waved goodbye to a rather reflective James. All of us wondered why he was not supposed to accompany us.

For Brother Andrew, the China of 1977 was an extraordinary change compared to the China visited in 1965. The averted look in the faces of the people had been replaced with a shy openness and a welcoming smile. Above all, Brother Andrew noticed that the people now seemed to have a hunger, a vulnerability, a need for something.

Mao had set himself up as the object of his own "religion." As Brother Andrew later wrote, "But now Mao is dead. Who will take his place? Deep inside, the people weep and wait. The earthquakes that rent their world threw them into panic. To whom will they turn? Not to themselves—Mao has killed love among them. To whom, then? I know of no nation in Asia with people so open, so desperate to accept the message of God's love."

Our Chinese hosts were very eager for us to attend one of their famous operas. We didn't disappoint them. The performance was a typical "art-form" of the government's propaganda machine. Twirling figures, brightly clad in red, extolled the virtues of Chairman Hua and the State, while at the same time they denounced the villains of the show: the "Gang of Four."

Since the opera was in Chinese, English captions to accommodate Westerners were projected on to a screen at the side of the stage. They were particularly revealing.

Wise Chairman Hua smashed the "Gang of Four" and shook heaven and earth.

"Heaven?" Julie whispered in my ear. "I didn't know heaven fitted into the communist's philosophy. . . ."

Chairman Mao delivers us from suffering. Mao was dead at the time, yet as the people's "savior," he continued to live on.

A third caption was equally disturbing: *On what basis should our policy rest? It should rest on our own strength and that means regeneration through our own efforts.* I looked at Brother Andrew. Would the religion of communism stop at nothing—not even regeneration?

And then the final caption was shown: *May the good news wing to all corners of the land.*

"Amen." Brother Andrew let out a deep sigh.

"Please, Lord," he whispered. "May the *good news* indeed wing to all corners of this land.

"Just look at these people," he said at last. "Whatever the State tells them to think and do, they comply with. This week they are to hate the 'Gang of Four' and smile at the *gwailos*. Last week we *gwailos* or foreigners were their enemies and the 'Gang of Four,' their heroes. What next?

"I am sure that if someone came on stage right now and told the Chinese to kill every white-skinned person in the hall, they would do it. They do not have a mind of their own anymore. They can't afford to. It's too dangerous!

"These people have become depersonalized automatons programmed by the government."

One morning Brother Andrew and I sat on a bench in a square in Guangzhou as crowds of people moved along. A number of friendly passersby shouted cheerful "hello's."

"Hi!" we replied.

Their smiles broadened. "Hi!" they repeated, copying the intonation in our voices.

"You have a lovely country," I called.

They nodded some more. "Lovey countee. . . ." Still smiling, they did their best to imitate the sentence though its meaning was lost to them.

The game continued for several minutes as the two of us called various phrases and the little group struggled gracefully to master the new words.

Before they left, we gave them the best phrase of all. "God loves you! God loves you!"

By now they were grinning from ear to ear. "Goh ruv . . . Goh ruv. . . ." If only they'd known what they were saying. If only, Lord. . . .

As we waved goodbye to them, Andrew's voice became serious. "David, the need here is great, and the people so ripe for the gospel. Now I can see more clearly than ever why the Lord has given us a vision for ten million Scriptures. But you are never going to make that target without more people helping you. You must find others willing to bring Bibles too."

"But that's no easy job," I replied. "Most people

think it's crazy to talk about a ministry to China right now. And more are frightened about what might happen if they got involved."

Nodding with understanding, Andrew nevertheless said, "But Jesus told us to 'go into *all the world*,' not just to those parts where Christians get the red-carpet treatment."

"Still," I persisted, "many people fear that even if they manage to get into China, they don't know what repercussions they might face inside."

"Then let me remind you of another point from that famous verse." Andrew leaned forward to make the point I have heard him repeat countless times since. "Jesus told us to *go* into all the world. But where does he say to come back again?"

For a moment, I couldn't answer him. Then, breaking into a hearty chuckle, I slapped him on the back.

"You're right, Andrew. Man, you're absolutely right."

"We think we should only go into a country if we can be sure of our return. Jesus never promised that," he said, wagging his finger in characteristic style. "Just think, David, when you were trained as a Marine, were you guaranteed a return if they sent you to war? No! Well, we are at war too— spiritual war. If we spend our time worrying about our safety, we will never get into the battle."

"But how can I ask that commitment of people?" I countered.

"Jesus asked for it. You just have to repeat His words. Anyway all around the world people are singing about the fact that they are going to heaven. If they believe that, what is their objection to getting there a little earlier?"

I had no answer to that one.

"Mark my words, David. Those who want to go into China for the Lord can and will do so. You just have to find them."

Because of urgent business, Brother Andrew left before our "drop" the next day. But as we saw him off at Guangzhou station, his contagious enthusiasm for the task remained with us.

A key verse from Psalm 57:2 was one we had claimed for every delivery of Bibles. It couldn't have been more apt for this delivery: "I cry to God Most High, to God who fulfills his purpose for me."

Right from the beginning of the transfer, we knew we had trouble on our hands. Six men had fallen in with the crowd behind our tour group.

We had agreed to meet our special "friend" in the park. As soon as I spotted the woman, I went to speak to her, only to find myself followed by one of the six men. After brief conversation, I casually drifted away, realizing the conditions for handing over the Bibles were impossible. We wandered around the picturesque park, while our "friend" observed at a distance. The six men were also keeping close tabs on us. I knew we were in for a very long afternoon.

With sundown approaching, we still had no idea how the Lord was going to "fulfill his purpose. . . ." All we knew was that we had to be very sensitive to His prompting when the time came.

At last, it arrived. A commotion had broken out a hundred yards away between two very angry men. Our followers, who were obviously secret police, rushed to the scene of the fisticuffs. They left us alone for the first time since our arrival in the park.

"David, your bag! Hurry!" Julie wasted no time. "I'm going to the 'comfort room,' and I'll need the tissues from the bag," she said, her eyes twinkling. I understood.

When our "friend" saw Julie walking towards the ladies' room, she too understood and quickly stepped inside. It was all unrehearsed, yet the

Holy Spirit had shown them what to do.

Before Julie reached the rest room, the policemen were back. They followed Julie to its entrance. From their vantage point they could see our group sitting on a park bench forty yards away.

Fifteen minutes ticked by. There was still no sign of the women. The policemen were getting restless, and so were we. Did the women intend to remain inside until the men left? How long would it be before they entered the public toilet, caught Julie and the woman with the packages, and possibly arrested them? "Lord, bring them out in five minutes, before the men get any bright ideas," I begged.

A minute after that prayer, Julie unexpectedly appeared near a little hill to one side of me. There was a big smile on her face. As she waved her hand, I could just make out a brief "one-way" sign. Obviously the transfer had been completed.

Fortunately, the policemen hadn't seen the other woman enter the rest room. They simply followed us all the way back to our hotel and then gave up.

What had happened inside the rest room? "There was a rear exit," Julie explained when we were in our hotel room. "We slipped out the back way, walked a few yards down a beautiful pathway there, and since the Lord had already seen to it that no one else was in sight, we made the exchange."

"So why did it take you so long?" I asked, conscious that she had been gone for over fifteen minutes.

"Well, it was very pleasant there," she replied matter-of-factly. "And with the transfer completed, we decided we had at least earned ourselves a cup of Chinese tea."

I smiled with relief. "You've got to be kidding!" was all I could say.

When I got back to Manila, James Wee was eager to hear all about our trip. As I shared it with him, the two of us wondered again why he hadn't been permitted to come with us. Then five months later, we got our answer. It came during another trip to Guangdong Province. James felt certain that the Lord had given him a green light for this more recent trip.

Once inside, James lost no time looking up his friend, Tan Hoc Tue. "Brother Tan, I wanted so much to visit you earlier this year but the Lord seemed to prevent my coming. Here, though, at last, I have brought your Bibles."

Brother Tan fought back tears as he lovingly examined each one. "I am glad that the Lord brought you at this time. It would have been wrong if He had allowed you to visit me on your last trip.

"You see, my brother," he continued, "I have been under close scrutiny by the authorities since that time." His face clouded with sorrow. "One of my children tried to escape just before that visit, but was caught and brought back here. Our family was immediately subjected to continuous observation."

"Were you harmed in any way?" James asked.

"No, but they knew about my being a Christian. During the time of Brother David's last trip, they took me to a nearby church to warn me off."

"Why did they take you there?"

Brother Tan gave a slight shrug. "They have photographs of believers who have been persecuted or imprisoned for their faith. They showed me these pictures and asked me whether I knew any of the people. Then they warned me, 'If you don't give up your bad ways, you will end up the same as these. Do you want that?'

"And so, my brother James, you can imagine

what might have happened if you had visited me then."

After recounting this conversation to me, James paused, knowing that his question had been answered. "It's like last time, Brother David," he said softly. "The Lord is one step ahead of us all the way. . . ."

FOURTEEN
THE YEAR OF THE TOURIST

"A young believer has managed to leave China. He's over here in Hong Kong!" Miss Woo sounded breathless over the phone. "How soon can you see him?" she asked.

Nineteen-year-old Daniel Kwang was the son of a woman with a remarkable ministry in South China. Reports of her work had already come to us via Miss Woo, our link between the believers in South China and the outside world. Through her, we had learned of an ever-growing revival often accompanied by signs and miracles akin to those of New Testament days.

Within twenty-four hours, I had arranged to visit Daniel at his grandmother's house in Hong Kong. A slim, shy-looking Chinese youth, he greeted us warmly. As we sat in the grandmother's living room, Miss Woo translated our conversation. Daniel told me his parents were well, sent me their love, and were also praying for me every day.

"The Lord is very wonderful in bringing me here," Daniel said. "You want to hear how He brought me?"

I nodded as he plunged into his story. On Christmas Day, 1975, the Lord had told him in prayer that he was going to leave China, and on a certain date should apply for his exit visa. Daniel had shared this information with his mother and a few other believers who kept it a secret and prayed about it regularly.

When the day actually came, over twelve months

later, he placed his application at the immigration office. The official behind the desk had heard all about Mrs. Kwang and the thousands she had brought to the Lord.

"Are you crazy? Who do you think you are, wanting to leave China? Of course you cannot go! Your mother is a criminal, an enemy of the State. Get out of here!"

In blind anger the official began beating Daniel on the face and body with his fists. When the man finally walked away, Daniel laid his case again before the Lord. "Last year, You told me this was the date for me to come. I don't understand what is happening. Please show me Your power."

At that moment, the man inexplicably stopped moving. Turning around to face Daniel, he asked in a new tone of voice, "Is your name Daniel Kwang?" The boy nodded *yes*. "And do you live at _____?" Daniel again nodded affirmatively, amazed at the change in the man. Without giving an explanation, the official had undergone a complete change in attitude. "Then," the man concluded, "come with me."

What accounted for the official's sudden favorable tone? At that time, about 300 believers had been meeting in Mrs. Kwang's home for fellowship and instruction. With the meeting over, they had disbanded and were on their way home. Suddenly the Holy Spirit stopped each of them and told them to return to the meeting and pray for Daniel immediately.

Mrs. Kwang was very surprised to see them all returning, each giving the same kind of explanation: "The Lord spoke to me saying that your son is to get his visa for Hong Kong. I have come to pray for him and give thanks."

Later that night, Daniel was given his visa papers!

As the months went by, Daniel told us more about the extent of the revival. At the same time, we were hearing accounts of revivals on a lesser scale in central and northern China as well. With each report, we understood more clearly the vision of ten million Scriptures for this colossal nation.

To date, however, we were so far from our goal that our efforts looked almost laughable. A few overseas Chinese and a handful of Westerners had been couriers delivering Bibles in quantities under fifty. At the same time, our couriers in the border countries were still journeying through the treacherous mountain passes into China. All of our efforts had hardly made a dent in the monumental task.

We now had contacts throughout China, just waiting to get Scriptures. But where were we to find the additional couriers to take them in?

The answer came unexpectedly early in 1978 when I was eating breakfast in Hong Kong. As I was reading the South China *Morning Post* one morning, a small advertisement caught my eye: "Tours to China!" These were being offered by a commercial travel organization, *not* by the China Travel Service. I recalled the number of times I'd tried to get into China over the past few years. An ad like this seemed an impossibility!

And yet, was it? We'd been watching for change in China since 1976, when both Chou and Mao died. According to what I had understood in Psalm 37 when I was at Far Eastern Broadcasting Company several years before, China would open up once the two leaders fell.

I also remembered the strange tale Daniel had told me about the day Mao died. He said, "During that afternoon, the sky became very dark in our area. Lightning and thunder came. It was so strong that the old people, even those in their eighties, said that they had not seen anything like it in fifty years. They came out of their houses and then turning to each other, said: 'The old man is dead. Chairman Mao has gone.' And they rejoiced.'' A little later, news from Beijing confirmed that the Helmsman had indeed died at that time.

Daniel then explained that these people believed, as so often happened in the Bible, that earthquakes signal a change of some kind. Thus, when China's devastating earthquake occurred in 1976, they were expecting a change in their country. Their leader's death, just one month later, only confirmed their expectation.

Another incident quickly flashed in my mind. Shortly after Mao's death, James Wee and I had been on a trip to Beijing. One morning I decided to take an early stroll around Tian An Men Square. Wearing a blue denim outfit and Mao cap, I stepped out into the vast square. Thousands of people in uniform lined up in three sections. They were patiently waiting to pay their respects to the deceased Mao.

As soon as I moved into view, thousands of eyes focused on me. I was the only foreigner in the square at that time in the morning. I smiled, but nobody smiled back.

I decided to join the long line of mourners. The wait seemed endless as the line slowly inched its way toward the crystal coffin, surrounded by its many "offerings" of brightly colored flowers.

I couldn't help wondering at the amazing hold that Mao, even in death, had over his people. Here were thousands still paying tribute to a man who, according to the *Guinness Book of World Records,* had been responsible for the deaths of more people than any other person who ever lived. More than Hitler . . . Stalin . . . Amin. . . . A man whose pictures had adorned almost every home, shop window, public building, and billboard. He had been the object of adulation, even worship, by millions of people.

When my turn came to stand before this giant of twentieth-century history, I saw a small, sallow, shrivelled body. The once full, red cheeks were now sunken and yellow. The dark eyes, formerly bright with ambition and power, were now shut. Even modern China's self-made god was no match for death, the greatest equalizer of all.

"If only Mao had known You, but You have Your plans and he was part of them," I prayed. "Lord, use this moment in China's history to lift the minds of your people here beyond their political 'father' to their one true Father. Bring them back to Yourself."

Now, in 1978, the extent of the change in the last two years since Mao's death had become more obvious. The China tour ad was just another indication of it. I asked Pastor Ward, one of my co-workers, to check into it.

Within weeks, staff workers from Asia and the United States had been booked on tours to Guangzhou and Beijing, Shanghai, and Nanjing. It seemed that 1978, in keeping with Chinese tradition, was indeed the "Year of the Tourist."

On each of the available tours, visitors who would be couriers were tightly screened and carefully prepared for the trip. They came from the United States, Australia, and New Zealand. The utmost caution had to be taken for the protection of the believers inside.

The teams were also counseled for their border crossings: "There is no way, humanly speaking, that we can outsmart communist officials. They are trained to perfection. The only way to get God's Word into China is to allow Him to do it for you. Your part will be to make sure you are walking close to Him so that you can sense His leading as He does so."

Their suitcases had no false compartments; the Bibles were simply placed inside. Then the tourists would be on their way with the well known prayer of Brother Andrew in their hearts:

Lord, in my luggage I have Scriptures that I take to Your children across the border. When You were on earth, You made blind eyes see. Now, I pray, make seeing eyes blind. Do not let the guards see those things You do not want them to see.

Time after time these tourists returned, thrilled by the way God had made "seeing eyes blind." Something always happened to distract the customs guards—just at the critical moment. It was never the same thing twice; the distraction was always different, and always outside of the courier's control. What remained the same was God's sovereignty in clearing the way of His Word to go through.

One of the first tourist couriers, Jim Cooper, had to face the rugged Shenzhen customs hall, a room divided into narrow compartments, with several customs men in each. The ratio of customs officials to visitors was strictly one to one. Jim was directed to an official at the far end of the room.

As he walked toward the man, another guard closer to Jim unexpectedly became free. The official at the far end then gestured for Jim to turn to the one nearby. Jim obeyed only to be told by that guard to return to the original one. Again, Jim followed instructions, but by now the customs officer at the far end was chuckling. He directed Jim to return once more to the other amused colleague. The two officials continued their game of Chinese "ping-pong" with Jim, who by now, was laughing along with them.

Eventually, Jim placed himself equidistant between the two. Putting his bags on the floor and his hands on his hips, he said, "Come on, fellows. We have to come to a decision about this. Others are waiting."

At his remarks, the guards laughed heartily and with a wave of their hands gestured for him to pass on, bags unopened. Jim gladly complied, inwardly marveling at not only God's sense of timing but obvious sense of humor as well.

We were very thankful for Westerners like Jim Cooper who were willing to be Bible couriers. However, we also needed more overseas Chinese with a burden for the church of their motherland. They could do so much more since they spoke the same language and looked similar to their fellow countrymen. How much more compassionately we could understand the suffering church through their face-to-face communication!

Peter Wong, a medical doctor in the West, was one of the first overseas Chinese to help us. He had relatives he'd never met and longed to deliver Scriptures to them.

His Bibles had been carefully packed in the middle of his clothes, while other items had been stuffed along the sides of the suitcase. When he arrived at customs, a young woman official checked his bags. It seemed as though her hands were guided; she placed them at the sides of the suitcase and on top of it. Then, as if still not sure, she pulled out one pair of trousers as far as the top of the leg. Before she got to the pocket in which Peter had placed several New Testaments, she seemed satisfied and pushed the pants back into the suitcase. Just one or two more inches and she would have found the Scriptures!

Once inside the country, Peter lost no time locating his relatives. He visited an uncle who had once been a dedicated Christian. During the Cultural Revolution, he had been demoted from a top-ranking professional in his field to a janitor—all because of his faith. Just recently he had been restored to the position his ability merited.

"Do you still believe?" Peter whispered to him.

"In my heart, yes, but I never speak to anybody about it," the uncle replied.

"You mean you have no fellowship?"

"None."

Another encounter with a relative was even more disheartening. Peter shared his testimony with a cousin who then revealed that he had been a Christian for three years prior to "Liberation," but that his beliefs were all different.

"After all, I hold a responsible position now," the cousin told him.

Peter couldn't believe he was telling the truth. "Has your faith really gone? Do you truly no longer believe?" Peter asked him.

The cousin seemed embarrassed and under strain. Instead of replying to the questions, he stood up and said, "We must get going now. You don't want to get back to your hotel late."

With China's door opening ever more widely, many more Westerners began pouring through. Bibles were still coming over the mountains from the border countries. Help for the suffering church in China was growing stronger week by week, month by month. We had ordered 20,000 Bibles from India and these had already begun trickling in from various border countries. Our team was also growing—Todd Martin was our newest member.

At the same time, more and more letters continued making their secret way out to us in the Free World. The sense of oneness these letters expressed touched us more deeply than anything else. Despite barriers of geography, culture, and ideology, the unity of the Body could not be broken.

One letter which I'll treasure all my life was written by Mrs. Kwang herself in the unmistakable language of the Chinese suffering church. In translation it read:

I have learned of your love for me, which touched me deeply and made my tears flow. Although this world is slowly changing, the love of my God does not change. Your love really comes from the Lord, which is forever, and the longer it gets, the deeper it becomes. This love refreshes me. Every time I mention your name in prayer, I can not help rejoicing and thanking God for you.

Paul said, "I count all things but loss for the excellency of the knowledge of Christ Jesus my Lord; for whom I have suffered the loss of all things, and count them but dung . . . and the fellowship of his sufferings, being made conformable unto his death . . . I might attain unto the resurrection of the dead."

My beloved! "They which run in a race run all, but one receives the prize. . . ." We are going to obtain an incorruptible crown. So, let us run together! . . .

"My God shall supply all your needs according to his riches in glory by Christ Jesus." Our family here loves you very much and greets you in peace.
Your cousin who always remembers you

My work was now requiring me to travel more and more. But what I enjoyed most about all the trips was returning home again. Julie had made it a tradition for the children to meet me at the airport, if they had no school the next day. My welcome at home would be warm nevertheless.

A large banner of welcome was sure to greet me

outside the house. If I'd been to a country in the Free World, the banner would be covered with appropriate words. Otherwise, they were careful not to give a hint of where I'd been.

There was no end to their originality, it seemed. The three D's sometimes greeted me with helium-filled ballons bearing the words "We love you, Daddy."

During one of my evenings home, Julie and I were reading our Bibles when Julie unexpectedly put hers aside. "You've been reading quite a large chunk of your Bible tonight," she said.

"Uh-huh," I replied, half absentmindedly.

"Do you realize that ten years ago you wouldn't have been able to do that?"

I put the Bible down slowly.

"I think the Lord's been working a slow but steady miracle right under our noses," she said.

When had the changes begun? At college, reading had still been a struggle for me, and it was only a little better after we were first married. "Maybe it really started to change after I met Jesus," I said. "Goodness knows, I've asked Him about it often enough."

"And all those hours you spent reading the Bible under Mr. Roy's direction," Julie mused. "Maybe the Lord used those, too."

We tried isolating the time of a major breakthrough, but couldn't. It had simply been a slow, quiet improvement that the Lord had given me through the years since I'd turned my life and that reading problem over to Him.

Even now, I was no speed reader. And reading in public made me uncomfortable. But that night I realized that the crisis of reading was now a thing of the past. God had brought me to the point where, instead of an obstacle to overcome, reading had become something to enjoy.

I recognized that even in my personal life, just as in the border crossings, God was accomplishing the seemingly impossible. And I felt deeply grateful.

FIFTEEN
SWEETER THAN HONEY

The little blue taxi drew to a halt outside the university in Guangzhou. Near the entrance stood a "welcoming committee," a jeep manned by two green-clad soldiers with loaded rifles.

Do they know all about me? Have they been expecting my visit? Do they know Mrs. Kwang is inside? Joseph Lee thought as he glanced out the taxi window.

Joseph, making his first trip to China in four years, was on his way to visit Mrs. Kwang, the woman evangelist whom the rest of our team longed to meet. Mrs. Kwang had been secretly staying with a doctor's family in the university to escape the authorities.

Joseph's youthful appearance helped him pass himself off as an overseas student. Inside the building, he asked for Dr. Chang and filled out a required registration card. *I am her brother in the Lord,* he thought and confidently wrote "relative."

Then he went to find Dr. Chang. The first person he met in the hall turned out to be the doctor himself! "I'm here to see Mrs. Kwang," Joseph whispered, and the two proceeded to Dr. Chang's quarters. His lodgings were relatively safe since university residents were not required to register their addresses with the local authorities.

When Mrs. Kwang appeared, the glow in her expression struck him immediately. Instead of the gaunt, even scarred, face which he'd expected to see, hers radiated love and tranquillity.

They spent five days meeting together, and he brought her fifty-six Bibles for her to distribute among her co-workers. "How many more do you need?" he later asked her. Her reply came as quite a surprise.

"Dear Brother Joseph, we could use, at the very least, 1,000 Scriptures."

When Joseph returned from his trip, Julie and I listened eagerly as he told us all about it. "I tell you, God is doing a mighty thing through that woman. The first thing I saw when I arrived at her place was a huge pile of mail, all from Christian leaders throughout the country. Mrs. Kwang is just a beautiful, motherly lady. In herself, she is not extraordinary. It's because she walks *so* close to Him that He can do a great work through her." Joseph paused briefly.

"She would stop her stories every few minutes, Brother David, to speak of the goodness of the Lord, and His care of her family and the believers. Really, her eyes were just alight for Him. She constantly exhorted me to trust in Him alone and to stand on His Word. Oh, her knowledge of the Scriptures . . ." he broke off, shaking his head, . . . "just fantastic!"

"So you don't have any doubts about her and her work?" I asked him. Several years before, Joseph had found such a ministry difficult to accept as authentic.

"But you haven't told us what Mrs. Kwang looks like!" Julie interrupted.

"Oh, Mrs. Kwang has black wavy hair, brown eyes, and a round smiling face in which you can almost see the presence of Christ Himself," Joseph replied.

Since her latest imprisonment, the evangelist had been sought relentlessly by the secret police. They wanted to imprison her again, this time for life. But amazingly, every attempt to find her had been unsuccessful. She told Joseph that, since that last time in prison, the Lord had promised her she would never have to face another arrest.

Clearly, subsequent events had proved Him faithful to that promise. Frequently, when she was holding a meeting, the Lord would warn her of danger and show when to bring a meeting to a halt, often just before the secret police had planned to raid the meeting place.

Mrs. Kwang's co-workers were also witnesses to miracles. One account of a co-worker whom the Kwang family affectionately called "the Old Man" touched us deeply. "The Old Man" had come from a very poor family and because of reading problems had been forced as a child to leave school. When the communists came to power, they made him chairman of their area and gave him a big house and double rations of rice to prove a point. But the man loved the Lord so much that he used his home for worship meetings and gave rice to hungry believers until he ran out.

When the authorities finally heard of his activities, they ordered him to choose between his faith and his new position. "I will not disobey my Lord," he told them. Once again, he became the poorest man in the area, without even a place to live. During these early days after Mao took power, the Christians were either too poor to help him or were imprisoned. One person did manage to provide him with a small room to use, but could not give him food. For several days he lived there on only water, until he became very weak.

Joseph continued telling us the story. "One morning he noticed a big hole in the wall and tried repairing it with a blockade of stones. But within a few hours, there was another large hole. He decided that it was somehow from the Lord. Later a large rat came through the hole several times, each time bringing sweet potatoes, nuts, and vegetables."

"For the old man to eat?" I asked.

"Yes, yes," Joseph repeated as if to get the message home to me. "The rat brought him food. Otherwise he would have starved to death.

"Every morning the rat came to him with enough food for that day. Sometimes, when the man was expecting someone else to visit him in the day, the creature would bring him a double portion of food."

"How long did this go on—a few days?" I asked, still incredulous.

"Several months."

I shook my head. Then Julie turned to me. "But honey, we accept all that for Elijah when he was fed by the ravens at the brook. Why couldn't it happen in twentieth-century China?"

I guessed it could, but it was still quite incredible.

Julie squeezed my hand. "How big is your God?" I smiled. God had already done so much in my own life. Surely I could trust him to meet the needs of others in up-to-date Bibleday style!

The final surprise came when Joseph informed us of Mrs. Kwang's request for 1,000 Bibles.

"But the most we've ever taken through Hong Kong is fifty!" I responded. *One thousand seems impossible,* I thought. *A delivery that size means biting off more than we can chew. What if it fails? How can we do it?*

In that question lay the key to my answer! *We* couldn't. That was the beauty of it. The Lord Himself would make the way. "I cry to God Most High, to God who fulfills His purpose for me," I finally said aloud.

Julie and Joseph nodded in agreement.

"If the Lord is going to have us bring ten million Bibles to China, it's no doubt time we started taking in more than fifty at a time," I said. Then I winked at Julie. "After all, He's the same God today that could feed Elijah by the brook. I guess we can trust Him for a thousand Bibles."

Much of the planning for the unprecedented delivery took place with Daniel Kwang in Pastor Ward's tiny Hong Kong apartment. For forty-eight hours, the team, consisting of James and his wife Lyn Wee, Beng, Julie, an overseas Chinese, and myself, prepared strategy. Joseph, our key team member, had suddenly become too ill to accompany us.

Yet hadn't the Lord told us to go? Despite the clear direction I believed God was giving us, I couldn't suppress doubts about the mission. Had I misread God? Was I jeopardizing the lives of those involved in the delivery? After praying into the night, I finally fell into a fitful sleep.

The following morning, the team assembled for final worship and prayer. Later, we arrived at Shenzhen, loaded with 900 Bibles in our suitcases. The remaining one hundred would follow in a later delivery. Each of us passed through without incident until it was James' turn.

The customs official opened James' suitcase and began searching inside. His fingers delved deeply and finally came to rest on the thin layer of clothing covering his Bibles. James broke into a cold sweat. He was sure the man had felt the books—there were so many of them.

"Dear Lord, protect Your Word. Stop him, Lord," James prayed. Suddenly, the man straightened up and pulled the lid of the suitcase shut.

"Please pass on, sir. Everything is in order." At those words, James felt tremendously relieved, to say the least.

Then after joining us to board the train for Guangzhou, he quietly related the Lord's protection at the border, and all of us paused to give silent thanks.

By now, South China's landscape with its cloudless blue sky had become a familiar sight to me and some of the others. The red soil and curved hills of Guangdong Province were backdrops for the hard working peasants with their wide-brimmed woven hats. Children ran about, pointing to the train. Buffaloes, their black skins glistening like wet umbrellas, splashed in the rice paddies.

The words from Jeremiah 32 came to mind as I gazed at the rustic beauty beyond the train:

Ah, Lord God! It is thou who hast made the heavens and the earth by thy great power and by thy outstretched arm! Nothing is too hard for thee!

"Not even 900 Bibles, Lord?" I whispered.

In Guangzhou, we noticed a subtle change had taken place between our last visit and this one. "The billboards and the posters, David. They've changed," Julie said quietly.

She was right. The attacks on the "Gang of Four" no longer dominated the scene. Instead, there was a new emphasis. A colorful campaign had been designed to reach into the drab lives of the people and lift their aspirations to a higher plane. The Party Central Committee had launched its crusade for the "Four Modernizations."

The government's aim was to bring China up to par with the Western world by the year 2000 in four different areas: agriculture, defense, technology, and industry. Mammoth posters, depicting the coming utopia, dwarfed the people of Guangzhou.

We were disturbed by one poster of the two giants of recent Chinese history. The solid, practical Zhou Enlai (Chou-En Lai) was set against a dream-like portrayal of twentieth-century life, replete with skyscrapers, jets, oil rigs, radio and television towers, and the ubiquitous red flag. Zhou held a scroll apparently describing the "Four Modernizations." Behind him stood an even larger figure in white: Mao etherealized by a shaft of light supposedly from heaven itself.

In the foreground marched thousands of Chinese figures, no larger than Zhou's fingernail. The tiny marchers wore bright clothes in stark contrast to the dull blue uniform of the real Chinese. Letters on the poster said the two leaders had given the "Four Modernizations" as their "grand behest."

The opening up of China had become even clearer to me now. Obviously to achieve its goals, the country would have to invite the Western nations to share their expertise. No longer could the Great Wall shut the People's Republic off from the rest of the world. In order to reach its target, China would have to woo the West and win it.

But once its needs had been met, what then? Would the honeymoon be over, and the nation once again turn its back on the Free World? Or worse, would it use that newly acquired progress against the other powers?

It suddenly occurred to me that we had no time to waste. The Lord, in His wisdom, had allowed China to embark upon its current program. The new openness was our ideal opportunity to bring spiritual food to the believers. We had to act, while we had time.

"Brother David, we don't have long now. It's time to get back." James' voice cut through my thoughts. "We must be on time to deliver our gifts!"

He was right. As we hurried off to organize the Bibles, I broke out in a cold sweat of nervous anticipation.

Julie and I prayed during the afternoon, while the others took taxis to deliver the Bibles to Mrs. Kwang's contacts. Once again our obviously

163

Western looks required that the two of us stay behind.

"Not a single hitch, Brother David," James told us a few hours later. "We set off for our destinations, and in no time had delivered all the Bibles."

That night we had a Chinese banquet to celebrate. We enjoyed fish, chicken, pork, and rice cooked a dozen different mouth-watering ways. We continued our conversation over lychees and Chinese tea.

"You know, David, this afternoon was so easy, almost too easy," James said. "I can hardly believe it!" His comment made me smile until I recalled another time at Tokyo Airport when those same words had cost us something. That was when we had missed out on our trip to China because of doubt. The incident was like a mirror to me now as I realized I too had carried doubts about the success of the present venture. I felt as though the Lord Himself had rebuked me. When He puts something together, He makes it not only possible, but in a real sense so "easy."

If He could deal with 900 Bibles this way, He could guide triple that number through. Why, oh, why hadn't I been able to trust Him with more?

Before the year was out, Joseph Lee made one other trip to China and got unexpected answers to some of the questions from his trip four years earlier.

His first surprise came when he returned to see his relatives in Guangzhou. On his last visit, when Joseph had spoken to them of the Lord, they had been polite, but indifferent. This time, they were more interested as each set of parents gathered to accept a Bible.

One of the uncles followed Joseph to another room. "Nephew," he said quietly, "I believe in God now. Listen. 'For God so loved the world that He gave His only begotten Son, that whosoever believes on Him should not perish but have ever-lasting life.'" He beamed proudly. "When you left us after your last visit, you wrote that down on a piece of paper for each of us.

"You see, Joseph, since that time, I have put it in my heart and prayed every day according to what you told me. And now, I have great joy in my soul. I am so grateful you told me about Jesus.

"Do you remember how chronically ill my two children were when you were here before?

"You told me, 'Jesus is alive and He can heal the children,' and so I tried it. One of my children had been sick with asthma, but the doctors could find no cure. The other was also very ill, and no medicine could help him either. Even myself, Joseph, I had migraine which would never go away. But after we prayed, the Lord healed all three of us! I believe in Jesus. Jesus is alive."

That incident, and many like it, left Joseph with a deep conviction that overseas Chinese Christians proved ideal evangelists in China. From that time on, Joseph was irrepressible. Whenever he met Chinese believers in the West, his challenge was always the same: "Even if you cannot bring Bibles to China, you should still go there. Why not? You'll be able to witness to your relatives. But," he would add with his warm smile, "how much better if you take in the Word of God too."

One man whom Joseph particularly wanted to see again in Fujian was Pastor Chai, who had wanted help getting his daughter out of the country. Joseph was very apologetic because he had tried to fulfill the request but had not had any success.

"Oh, there is no more need to try," Pastor Chai said, much to Joseph's astonishment.

"Why?"

"She has decided to stay. You know we have a

great revival taking place in our town right now, in fact in many towns in China."

When Joseph saw the radiance in the faces of both father and daughter, it was obvious that they had no regrets. That night, the extent of the revival became very clear. At Joseph's arrival, the pastor had scheduled a meeting of the same congregation with whom Joseph had secretly worshiped before.

Instead of the fifteen people he had met last time, at least sixty or seventy were present. The room was crammed to absolute capacity.

Pastor Chai explained that this was a comparatively small meeting. "There have been many conversions, especially among young people, but here in the city we have to keep the numbers small. Out in the rural areas where the communist authorities do not have such tight control, hundreds attend meetings at one time."

Joseph found the same pattern throughout his trip. Christian leaders in each town recounted extraordinary growth in the numbers of believers during the recent four years.

It was estimated that the church had increased by an unbelievable 400 percent since 1949. And eighty percent of the new believers were young people, below the age of thirty.

But with the enormous growth had come an equally great hunger for the Scriptures. "We must have Bibles, Joseph. These new believers desperately need the Word of God to grow."

Many requested the Union Version of the Bible, the traditional translation, akin to the King James edition of the West. Others preferred more modern translations for the needs of their region.

The range of versions available was increasing all the time. Their requests included *The Living Bible* in Chinese, the *New China Bible* published by Asian Outreach, the *Today's Chinese Version* published by the American Bible Society, and the *New Chinese Bible Commission* edition. It was the Union Version, however, for which we were most often asked.

There was a difference, too, in the choice of script requested. The age-old written language of the country had consisted of thousands of complicated characters. Chairman Mao, however, initiated the use of a new script, with fewer and more simple characters for the people to learn. Since the new script was being taught in schools, many of the young people had trouble reading Bibles printed in the old script. At the same time, older people were stumbling over the new script.

In each town Joseph took detailed notes of the version, quantities, and type of script requested. He was carefully following Open Doors' policy of taking in only what the believers have specifically requested.

The believers' profound and consistent hunger for the Word of God stirred him deeply. He had met one poor believer living in retirement, who pushed money into his palm and insisted, "This is so that you can buy more Bibles for my people when you leave here."

"No!" Joseph had exclaimed. "There are people in the Free World who can afford to give offerings. You keep this money."

But his protests fell on deaf ears. Finally, Joseph reluctantly accepted the money, pocketed it, and then brought it out again with a gentle smile.

"Brother," he said, "I have recently been given some money. I would like to donate it to you to pass on to your brothers and sisters in prison. Will you take it?"

"You see," Joseph told me later, "there just wasn't any other way that he would take it back again. . . ."

In addition to the believers' hunger for Bibles,

Joseph found their gratitude for Scriptures he delivered equally overwhelming. Often, to his embarrassment, they would insist on giving him something in return.

"But they could not afford to," he explained to me. "Many of them were on wages as low as forty RMB or twenty-five dollars per month. I did my best to dissuade them." But he was always unsuccessful.

Joseph was especially moved by one seventy-eight-year-old woman, who brought him a large jar of the best honey in the area. "This is my offering to the Lord," she told him.

"No, you must keep it! It is too valuable for you to give me!" Joseph protested, but the old woman wouldn't change her mind.

When he told me about that lady, I recalled the first trip I had taken to China via Rumania. After delivering Bibles to a pastor in Bucharest, I too had been the recipient of a thank-you gift of honey.

For me, the two incidents have added a new meaning to the verse from Psalm 19:10 in which David describes God's Words:

More to be desired are they than gold, even much fine gold; sweeter also than honey and drippings of the honeycomb.

SIXTEEN
THE BODY BROKEN

The law of the People's Republic unequivocally forbids any person who has been imprisoned to leave the country. Ever. Thus, when Miss Woo said the Kwang family might be coming out of China, we were amazed. Only a miracle could bring them out!

Daniel Kwang encouraged us to trust the Lord and then told us a story about his mother. "A long time ago, when my mother was in prison, the Lord told her that the whole family would one day leave China. They will come out. We just have to pray and pray."

That was precisely what he did. Starting often at 4:00 A.M., Daniel would pray for several hours before breakfast and then excuse himself to pray some more in his room. He prayed for his family, the believers in China, and for the Church in the West.

Brother Andrew and I had often discussed the need for intercessory prayer in this ministry. "David," he had told me, "we need to find people around the world who will become intercessors for the suffering church."

Even old Mr. Willis had once spoken to me about this kind of prayer in his Southern California home. "Tell me, lad, what does your prayer cost you? The Bible says that when Jesus was in Jerusalem, he wept over it. It also says in Hebrews that Jesus offered up his prayers 'with strong crying and tears.' Is that the way you are going to pray over your mission field?

"Mark my words, an intercessor is one who prays and weeps in the secret place of prayer until God stoops down and dries his tears."

The last ten years had taken me to that place many times on behalf of the millions in China who needed to know Jesus. Now it was time to be there again, to join Daniel Kwang in prayer for the safe exit of his entire family from the land behind the Great Wall.

Before long, God again showed us how much greater He is than any man-made system. He had prepared the Kwang family exit in an unquestionably miraculous way.

Four weeks before they actually left the country, the family had heard nothing about their visa applications, which had been filed several years earlier. However, one morning while in prayer, Mrs. Kwang sensed the Lord telling her that they would leave the country in one month's time. She would leave China to share the needs of Chinese believers with the world and to tell the world to prepare for Jesus' return.

In the meantime, she was told to instruct her coworkers for the month remaining, so that they would be equipped to carry on after she had left. When she informed the other believers, they were astonished. "That's impossible!" they protested. "No one can leave the country after being imprisoned. And you have been inside *three* times."

But the evangelist was sure her conviction had come from God. She spent the whole month teaching them, and on the final day commissioned each co-worker to continue the work.

The following day, a government official took the family to the police station to fill out exit papers.

While the Kwangs were filling out their forms the local authorities suddenly realized that one parent had been in labor camp and the other in prison.

"Wait a minute! Stop right there. *You* have no right to leave the country," shouted a clerk behind the desk. "Those papers will be ripped up immediately."

Commotion broke out and in the ensuing confusion, the Kwangs were asked to wait outside. A Christian who worked in the office later told them that while they were waiting, angry officials inside suggested soldiers be called in immediately.

Then, unexpectedly, the senior officer on duty announced that he had been one of Mr. Kwang's interrogators in labor camp. To the group's astonishment, he spoke up on his behalf.

"I called upon this man, time and again, to deny his faith," he told the men before him. "But he would not do so. Even in the face of death itself, he still would not deny his God." He gazed at the calm figure of Mr. Kwang. "I have respect for this man," he concluded quietly. Then, dispensing with the law of the land, he leaned across to sign the family's papers.

On their way out of the country, the Kwangs had to face yet one more obstacle. They had to travel by bus towards the border, but the route required them to make a ferry crossing. As they approached the water on the day of their trip, they saw a fog so dense that ferries could no longer pass through it. The family prayed that it would clear and so enable them to cross.

As the bus reached the pier, the fog began to lift. The ferry started its engine and the bus drove on board. After they had reached the other side, the Kwangs and the other passengers looked back. The fog had returned! They later learned that no more buses had been able to pass that day.

I was notified as soon as the Kwang family

arrived in Hong Kong. Eugene, an executive from Open Doors in the States, was in town at the time and accompanied me to Grandmother Kwang's house. I immediately recognized each member of the family. After all, I'd carried their picture in my Bible for eighteen months!

Tradition was put aside as they greeted us with open arms. Each of us had tears of joy and gratitude for this moment. Our interpreter was Ruth, a gentle European friend who spoke fluent Mandarin.

As our conversation unfolded, she translated stories about the suffering church inside. "The 'Old Man' sends you his greetings in our one Lord, Brother David," Mrs. Kwang said.

"As does all the 'family' there," added Mr. Kwang with a smile.

"When we heard that the 900 Bibles had come through, we held a meeting of praise and thanksgiving to the Lord. Tears ran down our cheeks," said Mrs. Kwang. "To us, it was like the time the children of Israel crossed the Jordan. The Lord has miraculously opened the way for His purpose to be fulfilled."

A look of shared joy spread from face to face as she spoke. In the flow of Chinese voices, I recognized just one phrase which I had heard Daniel use before: *Isan mei Chu* or *Praise the Lord*.

"And what are their current needs?" I asked, expecting them to name a figure similar to last time.

As Ruth softly translated their reply, she had no idea of the effect it would have on me.

"She says they need 30,000 Scriptures—immediately, Brother David."

It took me a minute to recover. I had just ordered that precise number three days before, not knowing that the Kwangs would be coming out at this time, let alone requesting such a delivery.

Thirty thousand Scriptures! What an enormous

load to consider taking to China at one time. One thousand had been overwhelming enough! But with the Lord's clear authorization, there could be no doubt that this was the next step for Open Doors in Asia.

"This has to be of the Lord," I said.

We discussed strategy for "Project Jordan" as it later came to be called among the staff. For security reasons, we also gave it a public name for Christians in the West: Project Rainbow.

The Kwangs told us that 30,000 Scriptures would satisfy immediate needs, but the overall need was for one million. This request was the first of that size we had ever received. If one family could ask for a delivery of this magnitude to meet the needs they knew of, how many more Bibles must be required by the many other groups throughout the country?

It was becoming ever clearer to us why the Lord had given the vision of ten million Scriptures for China. We began setting up research probes to find ways of fulfilling the Kwang request. At the same time we continued sending courier teams to other parts of China; meanwhile Eugene and I made several trips of our own together.

One of our trips called for a stopover at an airport in South China. An official guide named Chang Lo was assigned to accompany us during our wait. With briefcases and cameras, we set off for a mountain park in a car Chang Lo had booked in advance.

While I took off to photograph the beautiful scenery in the park, Eugene and the guide sat on a bench to admire the scenery. They talked at length in English describing their backgrounds, family life, work, and so on. Chang Lo was a university student; his parents were cadres in the community.

Eugene felt the Lord prodding him to witness to

173

the young man, yet wanted to resist the urge. He knew that if the Communist reported such a conversation, our real mission could be endangered. "Father, help me do the right thing," he prayed silently. "I'm not going to speak unless you make it plain that it's Your Will."

The conversation drifted to talk about the status of churches in China. Then, Eugene asked him cautiously, "Have you ever heard of a book called the Bible?"

Chang Lo had never read one in his twenty-one years, but when asked what he would do if he saw one, he replied without hesitation, "Oh, I would buy it."

"Why?"

"Because I like to read many books."

Chang Lo then asked about young people in the United States and even whether they attended church. Then he told a story about his English teacher from Great Britain. The man had told the class about a day when his house key was lost and how after he'd prayed, God had helped him find it. Eugene smiled, remembering the time when I, too, had lost some important keys.

"Do you believe my teacher's story?" Chang Lo asked. This was the opening Eugene had been praying for.

"Yes, I believe the story. That is just the way God works. Would you like to hear more about God?" With a wide smile, Chang Lo nodded affirmatively.

By the end of their two hours together, Eugene had talked about creation, God's love, Jesus His Son, and the plan of salvation. Finally, he asked him, "Can you believe, Chang Lo?"

"Yes, I can believe—just the way you told me."

Eugene then asked me if I had an "apple," our code word for *Bible*, to give Chang Lo. I gave him my personal copy.

At the airport, we told Chang Lo of the many brothers and sisters in Christ who would be praying for him. "God bless you," he said, placing his hands on Eugene's shoulders.

"I may never see that lad again," Eugene later said on the plane. "Correction," he added with a smile, "One day we'll meet in heaven."

During that year, Eugene and his wife Meg invited my oldest child, Deanne, to live with them in the States. She had graduated from Faith Academy in the Philippines and wanted a job in the States.

This meant that our family would have to be divided for the first time. Where would Deanne live? How would she cope in a different culture away from loved ones? These kinds of questions had churned around in our minds for some time. We should have realized that the Father who cared for us so faithfully loved our kids every bit as much as we. More so, in fact.

When Eugene offered to let Deanne live with his family, we knew it was an answer to our prayers. Deanne's work situation also resolved through the Lord's help. By day, she worked for a Christian organization closely linked with Open Doors. And by night, for many months, she took the role of night-nurse to Corrie ten Boom during Corrie's illness. And, in "Tante Corrie" she was privileged to find one more very special aunt.

"To think we feared she might be isolated and alone over there," I said to Julie one night. The Lord had shown that while He required us to live far from her, He could surround her with all that we had feared she would miss the most.

"The house will never be quite the same without her, will it?" Julie said. "I guess it will feel like this every time one of them leaves home." Julie's hands touched the fine gold chain hanging around her

175

neck. Deanne had bought it for her in the States. Suspended from it was a delicate pendant formed into the words: NO. 1 MOM.

A few months later during Easter Week, Eugene and I traveled to Beijing where we had already supplied believers with 300 cassette tapes of the spoken New Testament and gospel music.

On this trip we had additional tapes, four tape recorders, one hundred New Testaments, and several transformers for operating the tape recorders on local voltage. At customs, nothing was touched; no questions asked. We went through with a word of welcome.

Before delivering our "gifts," we'd planned to meet John, a European who spoke fluent Mandarin and was also our main contact there. Ever since our first meeting in 1978, the year before, we'd been delivering him Bibles. He lived in a place shared with others and so was storing the Bibles on the floor under his bed.

"But I have had no fear of being found out," he told us when we met this time. "I know the prayer Brother Andrew uses as he takes Bibles into communist countries. 'Lord, make seeing eyes blind.' And I've asked Him to do the same for the books under my bed. I have absolute confidence the Lord will keep my hidden books safe."

"And has anything been found?" I asked.

"No, nothing," John said smiling.

From John, we gained further insight into the broken Body of Christ in China and the traumatic extent of the wounds inflicted on it.

"Many have now reached the point where they no longer feel able to attend worship meetings," he told us. "They know that if they congregate in groups larger than two or three people, they run the risk of being charged as 'subversives.'

"Some are frightened even to visit other Christians, if those believers have been bold in expressing their faith. They are worried that the black mark placed against their brethren will also brand them.

"During times of extreme persecution," John explained, "some believers reneged on their faith and were coerced into exposing their fellow believers. The betrayal took the form of participation in 'struggle and criticism' meetings, or of helping the government draw up charges of counterrevolutionary activity by the Christians. Other believers cooperated with the government without meaning to. They were just too naive to realize the implications of their actions."

His expression hardened a little. "Of course, there were also those who had been impostors all along. These people were planted in the churches by the communists. They've caused great damage. Their method was to draw unsuspecting believers into positions where charges of illegal activity could be laid against them.

"I'll never forget the words of one believer who shared his pain with me. 'Persecution and physical suffering are terrible,' he told me, 'but to be betrayed by other members of the Body of Christ is the most bitter of all.'"

Of course, this pattern had been repeated throughout the country, but the wounds were taking longer to heal in Beijing, where the intensity of government restriction had eased only slightly during the post-Mao era.

John also told us about one woman who had already lost half of her family to prison and death by the time she was assigned to a labor gang. Her duties had been to break up rocks and to build roads. Day after day, the toil had drained her strength, leaving only bitterness and pain.

Finally one morning she felt she could no longer continue and wondered if the Lord was going to let her die. At that moment, she turned her head and saw an old woman she had never seen before.

"Do you still believe?" the woman asked her.

"I, I still believe," the believer nodded, almost unable to form the words.

"A bruised reed shall he not break and smoking flax he shall not quench," the old woman said, quoting from Matthew 12. Then, she turned away and walked out of sight.

After those words, the believer's heart began to lighten. She felt the strength of the Lord flowing into her. It was as if the Lord had given her a sign that He would not allow her to be broken completely through persecution.

That night, she diligently inquired about the old woman, but no one seemed to know her. The visitor had come and had just as mysteriously disappeared.

Another believer suffered unforgettable humiliation at the hands of the Red Guards during the Cultural Revolution. They had dragged the man from his house and had hung a sign around his neck which read: "_____is a bastard." They had incited others to taunt him.

Agonizing with shame, he had pleaded with the Lord for deliverance. "Why am I suffering like this, Lord? Please release me from it. I cannot bear much more."

At that moment, one of the jeering guards shouted, "Hey! This man is not suffering nearly enough. I have a better idea. Why don't we take the sign off and replace it with another one that says: *Jesus Christ is a b*_____?"

The Red Guards laughed with hideous glee as they carried out the suggestion. The believer felt his heart ready to break. "To suffer for you, Lord, is terrible, but this humiliation on your name is too much. . . ." He wept as the hatred around him grew.

Suddenly he sensed the presence of the Lord. It was as if Christ Himself had come to bear the mockery and pain in his place. And then he understood: Christ *has* borne our sin and shame on the Cross; Christ *has* taken away our pain and death.

"You see," John told us, "despair has touched the lives of many believers here, yet the Lord has reached out and strengthened them Himself. Some are weak; some are strong. Some have fallen away, while others have endured great suffering and emerged still believing. But they are not unscathed. Many hearts faithful to the Lord still bear the scars of anguish and anger against those who have damaged them.

"Yet, when they come to realize that there are others in the Body of Christ worldwide who care for them and love them, they are touched to their deepest core. A Bible placed in the hands of a believer has caused tears to flow. They say, 'The Lord has not forgotten us.'"

John concluded his report with a picture of the "above-ground" Christians meeting in China. The registered church in Beijing had recently undergone major changes. The Three-Self Patriotic Movement, obscured during the stormy years of 1966-76, had been revived early in 1979. And the Beijing Three-Self Church on Dong Dan Street had begun to show evidence of the change in atmosphere.

The regular attendance had increased beyond the forty there had been in February. Sermons and more fervent prayer had been introduced. Foreigners still made up the bulk of the congregation, but now more Chinese were beginning to attend. Clearly, we were witnessing the birth of China's new openness on religious matters.

After our meeting, John and a Chinese Filipino who had come with us transferred the "gifts" we had brought to their destination. When the delivery was completed, they were given a dozen hot, freshly-boiled eggs still in their shells. Knowing what this gift must have cost, the pair protested that they could not accept it, but the believers insisted.

"Please tell our two brothers that we are praying for them and are so grateful for the love they have extended to us. We, the Church in Beijing, cannot allow our brethren from the West to go empty-handed."

The following morning was Easter Sunday. Eugene, a Chinese friend, and I met with John soon after sunrise. Together we traveled thirty miles north to visit the Ming Tombs, where thirteen majestic "shrines" stand with their curved roofs golden in the sun, and walls a deep red. The cloudless sky was a rich azure, with just a hint of wind among the pines and juniper trees.

The four of us gathered in a secluded spot to remember the "broken Body of Christ" in China. The Lord's presence was very real to us as we worshiped together during that communion service.

We sat among the ancient tombs, housing some of history's dead emperors. Each tomb was a monumental demonstration of its ruler's quest, of man's quest, for eternity.

Then, by those shrines, we bowed our heads before the Living Christ, whose resurrection believers all over the world were also celebrating. Taking the eggs as the bread, we "broke and ate them." Our wine was the people's drink in China, "Pearl River Orange." We concluded our "service" with the words of the Lord, "As often as you do this, do it in remembrance of Me." We were also doing it with China in mind. . . .

SEVENTEEN
THE LION AND THE LAMB

With my most recent China trip behind me, it was time to work on Project Rainbow. At home, I faced the awesome prospect of getting 30,000 Bibles through. Then as the date of the delivery was approaching, I had an unexpected call from Hong Kong. It was Joseph Lee.

"Project Rainbow is in danger, Brother David! There's no way we can get 30,000 apples delivered under current weather conditions. There's been an unexpected change in the winds."

I knew there was no way Joseph could describe the "change in the weather" over the phone. "Hold everything!" I told him.

"Perhaps we could take on a smaller project instead?"

"Wait, I'll be over on the first available plane," I told him, reassuringly.

Project Rainbow was already well underway when he called. One major answer to my prayer had been the establishing of a prayer force throughout the world to pray for Rainbow. We hadn't described the project, but had simply asked them to pray for it daily.

In the United States alone, 90,000 prayer letters had been sent out. We knew that in Australia and New Zealand, 10,000 people were interceding for us. Even beyond our immediate locale, thousands more were prayer partners in Great Britain, the Netherlands, Africa, and Latin America.

One woman in the States told us she had been awakened in the middle of the night and been told by the Lord to pray for something called "Rainbow." She prayed obediently without knowing what it was all about at the time.

Besides the prayer partners outside China, there were those on the inside praying and mobilizing for Project Rainbow. They had prepared a comprehensive line of delivery to transport the Bibles once they arrived in China. Deliveries were also planned. Everything had come together so well, it seemed. So, how could the Lord be stopping us now?

When I arrived in Hong Kong, I found the reason for Joseph's worry. A courier, recently traveling with a load of Bibles into China, had found it impossible to deliver his cargo to its destination. He had been painfully aware of the ever-watchful eye of communism. Security inside had been tightened. Thus oppressed by the tension of his mission and the atmosphere, the courier had returned across the border with his Bibles intact.

"Perhaps we should think again, Brother David," said Joseph. "If we take in maybe half that number, we can do it in smaller amounts. It will be less noticeable. Then gradually, in time, we can send in more."

"But 30,000 is the number God gave us," I replied. We were sure this was to be our next delivery—ever since the Kwangs' exit from China. It was the express request of the family to meet an urgent need. And it matched precisely the number I had ordered immediately prior to their arrival.

If Satan was bluffing us now, we still had to stand against him. "I believe we should proceed as planned," I told Joseph. "But I'll tell you what. Why don't we put a fleece before the Lord? I'll ask Julie and the children if they'd be willing to act as couriers.

"If they're willing to go, and the Lord allows *them* to have a safe delivery even at this time, we'll take that as His authorization for Rainbow to go ahead."

"Won't they need a Chinese team member?" Joseph asked. "Where will they find one?"

"We'll let that be the final confirmation from the Lord," I said. "We'll trust Him to provide one for us." I smiled. "I believe He will, though."

One week later Julie, Dawn, and David arrived in Hong Kong. Although their tickets to China were booked, they as yet had no Chinese teammate—and it was only twenty-four hours until their departure. If the Lord did not provide one, their trip would be off. And, according to our fleece, Project Rainbow would have to be abandoned, and a much smaller delivery undertaken.

Late that afternoon, Mark Tao, Joseph's assistant on the team, met an old friend along Kowloon's Nathan Road. "I was going to call you today. I have to go into Guangzhou tomorrow. I thought I'd let you know in case there is anything you need done there."

With their new Chinese friend, Julie and the children entered the People's Republic. As if to prove to us that He was in control, the Lord let our kids carry out the transfer of Bibles with the Chinese team member! Although the experienced senior member of the team, Julie "happened" to be called by another Westerner to help with an urgent personal problem.

Later when asked how it had felt to make the delivery, my son David confidently said, "The Lord made it real *easy*." There was that word *easy*, again. And it was related, as in all prior instances, to ventures in which God had shown Himself so fully in control that everything had fit together perfectly. And easily.

Once more, Satan had been bluffing us. Project Rainbow was meant to proceed as planned.

The funds had all come in, the Bibles were paid for, and the couriers were making preparations. Only last-minute arrangements inside China remained to be finalized. This task fell to Joseph and Mark who had set off for a month's journey to complete the master plan for Rainbow. Concurrently they took the opportunity to check out the needs of believers in other parts of China. It was a two-fold expedition.

Traveling in the southern and coastal regions of the country, they were impressed by the overwhelming evidence of China's ever-widening revival. In the cities where control was tighter, they found meetings with as many as one hundred people. Rural meetings were often attended by several hundred or even 2,000 at a time.

In northern and inland China, away from the eye of the tourist, the authorities could take whatever measures they liked, with little chance of news leaking to the West. Some Christians in several provinces were still in labor camps, while tight restrictions were placed on any Christian activity in the cities.

Joseph and Mark were, thus, not surprised to find small meetings in the urban north. In Beijing itself, groups no larger than six were the norm. On the average, groups of between three and ten met in the towns.

However, there were places in the rural areas with meetings of up to a thousand people. Joseph told us that in one province there are one million Christians!

"These Christians have made a profound impact on their province," he said. "Do you know that they are so conscientious in their daily work

184

that their output has exceeded the quotas—and many communist officials have become Christians through their witness!

"Also, the believers can sing in their home services at the top of their voices. All one thousand of them, if they like. No one minds a bit," he told us. "And once when they held an evangelistic meeting, they borrowed the P.A. system from the communist officials!" Joseph laughed at my look of astonishment.

"Praise the Lord, Brother David. This revival is *His* doing."

It was just as the believers had predicted and prayed about for so many years. Thousands, even millions, in all parts of the country had become dissatisfied with the emptiness in the "religion" of the State, and were turning to Jesus. Brother Andrew had anticipated it too.

He once had told me the story of the lion and the lamb.

"Tell me, David, if I let a lion and a lamb loose in my garden, what will happen?"

"I'd give the lamb five seconds," I had replied.

"Aahh. But suppose I separate them first, then starve the lion while I feed the little lamb, and finally wait until the lion is too weak to raise his head. If at that time I let them loose again in the garden, what will happen?"

"Not much, I guess."

"You're wrong, brother. The lamb would be victor. If he wanted to, he could even step on the lion and proudly proclaim himself the conqueror.

"You see, David, the lion is the State, and the lamb is the suffering church of Jesus Christ. If we feed the lamb, it will become strong. And the emptiness of atheism will, in due course, come to an end—as the people discover the moral and spiritual vacuum in the system of the State. And so the lamb will conquer."

I then turned to Andrew with a smile. "Now, I understand," I said. "*That's* why Jesus said, 'Feed my lambs. . . .'"

On behalf of Project Rainbow, Joseph and his assistant, Mark Tao, had also spent some time in China, visiting believers who would be working with us.

On their travels, they carried a number of New Testaments to give away. By the time they'd reached Nanjing (Nanking), only five remained. They also had a very large Bible complete with concordance and references—suitable for a pastor. As yet, however, they hadn't found the person they felt God wanted them to give it to.

They decided to visit the home of a Christian woman in Nanjing, but were greeted instead by two young men whose shabby clothes revealed their poverty. Joseph and Mark were, nevertheless, quite impressed by their obvious love and radiant faces.

"We believe the Lord has a Bible waiting for us somewhere here," one of them said. "We know that the lady of this house sometimes has a supply of them. She's in Shanghai trying to get some now, and we are waiting for her return."

"How did you get here?" Mark asked.

"We came by two trains. It's been several days since we set out," the older one replied.

"Where did you sleep along the way?" Joseph asked them. By now, he felt fairly sure these men were genuine Christians, but he wanted to keep the conversation going a little longer until he was positive.

"We could not afford to stay in hotels. We just slept on public benches or on open ground," replied the younger man.

"Brothers," Joseph began, "we have two New Testaments we could give you." He moved toward his briefcase and the two followed him. Opening it gingerly to remove the Bibles, he tried to keep the lid down and the large study Bible out of sight.

Then, as he began shutting the case, both young men grabbed the lid in their eagerness to see inside. Joseph again tried closing it, but without success. The two pulled the lid open and caught a glimpse of the large Bible.

"Please, may we have that one?" they begged. "Please?"

As Joseph withdrew the Bible, he told them frankly his intention to give it to a pastor. "Will you make me a promise? Will you give this to your pastor when you return?"

The men smiled in agreement. Then during further discussion, Joseph learned that the older believer held meetings with around 800 in attendance.

"You're the one!" Joseph then told him with delight. "This was intended for you all along. Keep it, and may the Lord magnify your ministry."

Deeply challenged by the commitment of the two, Joseph and Mark discussed the believers' needs for Scriptures and promised that we would get several hundred Bibles to them as soon as a delivery system could be set up.

Later, Mark and Joseph reported to me that they were more convinced than ever that we were walking in God's will and that the 30,000 Bibles for Project Rainbow *had* to be delivered. The necessary delivery lines had been confirmed during that trip, and the enormous needs of the country had been reinforced for them a hundred-fold.

All was ready for the countdown to Project Rainbow.

EIGHTEEN
THE SMILE ON THE FACE OF THE TIGER

"Bibles! These are Bibles," the customs official said importantly. "You spell that B-Y-B-L-E-S. And you must leave them here."

His words sent a shock wave throughout the Project Rainbow network. Several thousand Scriptures had just gone through, but now two Bible delivery loads had been discovered at customs. After all the confirmations from God, was He telling us to quit?

Our couriers were forced to leave their Bibles at customs until their departure from China. However, a few days later, in Hong Kong, the Bibles were repacked in different suitcases and taken straight back inside the country.

We'd realized the perils involved. Moving 30,000 Scriptures behind the Bamboo Curtain placed every courier in a vulnerable position. But our greatest concern was for the believers inside who were risking their freedom and very lives to distribute the "apples" they received.

As with all our deliveries, the believers knew that if problems arose, they had only to give the word, and the project would be halted immediately. They had made the request for Bibles in the first place, so despite our mobilization efforts, they had the right to stop the project at any time.

Thus, as soon as he learned that some Scriptures had been found, Joseph informed his link-man among the believers. The mutual decision was to pray. No one knew what to do next.

During the night Joseph had a dream of our

Bible storeroom in Hong Kong being completely empty.

That dream served as another confirmation to continue with Project Rainbow. When he shared the dream with one of the believers, the man said, "Joseph, God is encouraging us. If that warehouse were empty, there is only one place the Bibles could have gone—here. I believe that is the answer to our prayer."

By the end of their time together, both were sure that the Lord was saying, "Go."

The rest of the delivery continued unhindered. After several days, two-and-a-half tons of Scriptures were carried by hand through the Chinese border. The final crossing involved Eugene, Shan, an American named Mason, two overseas Chinese, and myself. It was no easy thing carrying the heavy load of Scriptures across the border. The task was not made any lighter by the fact that Shan had broken his arm a few days earlier. It had been set in plaster and was supported by a sling.

Yet I came to give thanks for both, for during the customs check we nearly found ourselves in trouble. Eugene was chosen for close questioning by an official who held Eugene's visa in one hand and asked him to open his bags.

"I hurt my arm just recently," Shan suddenly said to the official, "and it is still giving me a lot of pain. I will need to sit down very soon. Can you show me where to find a seat?" With that, the official lost interest in Eugene, handed him his papers, and waved him on his way.

The rest of the Bibles went straight through without a hitch. Mason and I helped the women couriers with their bags. In each instance, the guards chatted with us briefly and sent us on. Their attention "happened" to be diverted elsewhere.

We knew that the ease with which this was happening had *nothing* to do with us or with our own cleverness. We were seeing God at work, once again making seeing eyes "blind." There was almost a timelessness about that moment, as though we were all part of something much bigger and greater than ourselves. And we were. Again the Psalmist's words echoed in my mind: "I cry to God . . . who fulfills His purpose for me."

Nonetheless, as the suitcases were being loaded for delivery to our hotel, I suddenly felt overwhelmed. The enormity of the operation, from a human viewpoint, had come home. Passing so many Scriptures through at one time, without hardly a ruffle of suspicion at customs, had been a challenge we'd never before attempted.

Almost without realizing it, I found myself confessing, "Lord, I never want to go through this again. Never!" Then, shamefacedly, I prayed, "I'm sorry, Father—after seeing You at work so clearly this afternoon. If You really want me to, I'll go through with it. But it will have to be in *Your* strength alone."

At the hotel, I slapped Shan on the back. "Do you realize," I said delightedly, "the Lord even had a purpose in your broken arm? He brings every little detail together to achieve His purposes. Praise God!"

"Amen to that," Shan responded. "All things *do* work together for good. . . ." By now he was sitting down and nursing his painful arm. He glanced up at me with a look of mischief on his face. "But next time, David, if we need a limb broken, we'll make it yours, all right?"

Now that we had brought the Bibles into the country, we had to wait for their distribution to the Chinese Christians themselves. At times, the seriousness of the situation threatened to overwhelm us as the thousands of Bibles continued to find their way into the hands of believers.

Those involved in the line of delivery needed great sensitivity to the Spirit's leading every time they ventured from one home to another with a Bible. Our role was to support them by praying that there would be no problem with even one copy of the Scriptures.

At last word came: All the "apples" had been taken safely to their destinations without a single loss.

The delivery of that news came in a surprising form: a delegation of three Chinese believers standing outside my hotel door. They held dried figs, hand-embroidered table cloths, and a sheaf of Christmas cards.

As I welcomed them into the room, I found it hard to believe this was really happening. With security risks so great, none of the Christians had ever dared visit a team of Westerners before. Spies were all over. The government even had their people posted on each floor of every hotel!

"The church wants to thank you. We are here to let you know what you mean to us," the believers said, passing around the dried figs.

They stayed with us for two hours. During that time they related the pressures they were facing, but most often spoke of the goodness of their Lord. We linked hands in a circle and prayed—East and West joined as one. I knew I was fellowshipping with some of God's choicest people.

As they were leaving, they hugged each of us on the team. When I told them I was still amazed that they had come out so boldly to see us, the leader replied, "It was nothing. Our mighty God walked before us. It's not only the customs officials whose eyes He can make blind. We were not even followed! Praise the Lord, Brother David."

"Amen. God bless you richly, brother. Tell the family that we and thousands of prayer partners in other countries are praying for you all."

Eyes moist, he clasped my hand tightly in both of his. "Tell them we are praying daily for our brothers in the outside world too. Tell them we love them and never cease to give thanks for their gifts. Make sure they know, Brother David."

With the Bibles now safe at their destinations, we spent our remaining time in China in the expected role of tourist. Doing so, we saw yet another development in the series of ever-changing faces of the country.

The billboards, as usual, heralded the change. We still saw occasional signs urging the people toward the Four Modernizations, but we saw many more promoting material good. Watches, color televisions, sewing machines, and fans were advertised in place of political posters. Even Western cigarettes were being promoted in the center of the city.

One evening I walked down the streets I had trodden with James Wee a few years earlier. The ageless quality could still be felt. There was, however, an all-important newcomer—television. Every second or third house had a set, displayed in a place of honor in the living room. Often close by could be heard a modern electric fan whirring proudly. In other rooms, distinctly Western music was coming from many brand-new cassette recorders. These three items were obviously the longed-for possessions of every householder.

How could the people afford such luxuries? In order to get maximum work efficiency from the people, the government had introduced a system of monetary incentives. Communes competed with each other for the greatest productivity. Within each commune, the workers who labored the longest hours and achieved the most earned more points than the others. And more points meant more pay. Each was granted a private plot of land to grow crops to sell at the market. Factory workers were divided into teams and were urged to compete against one another. Again, the best team received the best pay.

"Not that our people lack anything," our guide hastily explained, "but if they know they can earn a little extra money this way, it helps them work harder. Then our country can progress further along the road to modernization, like your countries in the West."

At that moment I sensed how fundamental a change was underway in China. In order to achieve its program, the country had had to give its people new motivation. Had it also given them a new god every bit as powerful and influential as their recently deceased one? Was Mammon the new god of China?

Some months later, we saw further confirmation of my thoughts. Chairman Hua, the handpicked successor to Mao, stepped down from his position as premier of the country. On his death, the Great Helmsman Mao had chosen Hua to follow him because of his adherence to a hard Maoist line of thought. In contrast, the new premier, Zhao Ziyang, had been schooled by Deng Xiao Ping himself in the politics of pragmatism.

With Zhao in power, China's future would be steered more than ever toward the Four Modernizations. This then was more than just a change in personnel. Mao was slowly but surely to be toppled from his pedestal and Mammon called upon to unite the country for its golden future.

As tourists, many of the other team members in Project Rainbow had opportunity to visit the increasing numbers of Three-Self churches opening up in the major cities of China. Reports of China's new policy of religious freedom had already reached the international press.

In that year of 1979, people around the world were asking why the People's Republic had suddenly reversed its position on religion. Not only had the Three-Self Patriotic Movement been re-established, but also the Catholic Patriotic Association, the Chinese Islamic Association, and the Buddhist Association. Reasons for encouraging such groups were gradually becoming clear.

The current leaders wished to harness all energies toward the fulfillment of their new goals. Therefore, to a certain extent, philosophical differences of opinion could be overlooked in order to consolidate all groups in the country behind a united front.

Far more important, though, was China's new need for Western technology. Modernization would never be achieved without it, and the communists knew such expertise would not be given unless they demonstrated respect for the individual's right to belief.

Thus churches began opening in the major cities of the tourist belt. There travelers could observe the new churches and so carry impressive reports about the new freedom back to their various homelands.

Whatever the government's reasons, and however long this new relaxation was to last, grateful believers in the thousands were worshiping in the new found freedom of the officially sanctioned Three-Self churches.

That year of 1979 also brought my old friend Pablo to work full time with us at Open Doors. He and Todd Martin played strategic roles in Project Rainbow and seized the chance to visit an official church together.

They noticed, as did all our team members, that there were very few Bibles in the churches. After a church service, Pablo approached one of the pastors to discuss the scarcity of Bibles. He'd observed this man earlier and had felt a spiritual oneness with him.

As the two talked in private, Pablo asked if he would like a copy of *Decision* magazine in Chinese. The Pastor gratefully accepted it, and then Pablo carefully broached the subject of Bibles.

"How is the situation here? Do you have enough Bibles or do you need more?" he asked.

The pastor lowered his voice. "We need them *very desperately*. Anything we are brought, I would be glad to accept."

Pablo's question had been basically one of research for the future. Much as he longed to help meet that need, he knew that at this stage, it would be foolish to deliver any Scripture loads directly to the Three-Self Church.

After talking with a number of other pastors, they noticed a man with whom they felt no sense of unity at all. In fact, they strongly suspected him to be the official Three-Self "eye" in that church.

During their discussion, Todd, in his own diplomatic way, said, "You know, we have a lot of Christian Chinese friends in Hong Kong. And they're always wondering what they can do in a practical way for their brothers and sisters. What can we tell them? They were wondering, for example, if you would need Bibles."

The man our team suspected was from the Three-Self movement replied with a resounding "No!" Then he spoke in Chinese to the same pastor who had previously spoken to Pablo in private. The expression on the pastor's face was completely impassive as he translated the message: "*He* says to tell you, 'We have no need of Bibles in China.' *He* also says to tell you we are printing our own Bibles next spring and we will have adequate supply. Therefore, we don't need any."

Brother Andrew had already prepared us for this type of response. He had told me, "The problem between official and unofficial distribution is that usually no matter how many copies a communist government is prepared to print or import, you can be sure in every case the supply is a long way short of the demand. Maybe a trickle of Scriptures will be supplied to a population, but they still desperately need many more to come in unofficially. The believers heavily depend on unofficial couriers for their supplies. So we should not disappoint them."

How many Bibles would the government need to print simply to replace the hundreds of thousands burned during the Cultural Revolution? And if, just supposing, they *were* ever replaced, how many more would be needed to accommodate the 400 percent increase in the population of the Chinese church?

One fact should not be forgotten. An intrinsic part of all communist ideology is atheism. Therefore, when such a government speaks of religious freedom, its claim needs to be examined closely.

Joseph gave us a list of topics which Three-Self pastors must avoid in their sermons. These topics were given behind the scenes to ensure that pastors do not infringe party policy.

The topics included:

● *Tithing*. (This would affect the economy.)
● *Day of rest: Sunday*. (This would affect production.)
● *Healing and exorcism*.
● *Marriage between believers and unbelievers*.
● *The Second Coming of Christ*. (This might undermine the people's single-mindedness toward the Four Modernizations.)

Preachers are not allowed to address communist officials, nor are they supposed to evangelize young people under the age of eighteen.

One young girl, the daughter of a Three-Self pastor, summed it up succinctly. "My father really loves the Lord, but feels as though he is preaching with his hands tied behind his back."

Clearly then, there is considerable discrepancy between the government's claims of religious freedom and the reality of the situation. One of the senior administrators, working under Bishop Ting, chairman of the Three-Self Patriotic Movement, recently expressed his frustration, "I am sick of being a puppet for the government and of having to repeat the same lies. I'm just about ready to tell the Bishop so."

The Three-Self movement package is unquestionably bound by the communist government's red tape. But the people who make it up are a different matter. "You can't know for sure," John had told me in Beijing. "All kinds of people make up Three-Self churches.

"Some are certainly fakes, planted by the government to spy on others. Some have succumbed to the pressure of the government and have compromised their faith, knowingly or unknowingly, in the party's interests. Others are genuinely doing their best to worship their Lord and serve His flock in a situation of compromise."

Compromise. Even at best, the believers who went along with the government church knew they had to compromise. It was the same throughout the other restricted countries.

There is thus a kind of suffering within the Three-Self system—suffering which can only find its solution in the love of Jesus.

Thousands, probably millions more, however, have chosen to stay away from public worship.

Mee Lei, an overseas Chinese girl, met one such believer, a middle-aged woman.

She said, "Those who attend church regularly have to register their names and addresses. That's what happened before the Cultural Revolution, too. And then when the authorities wanted to persecute us, they knew exactly who we were and how to find us. Most of us are not prepared to take that kind of risk again."

"Well, is there any *real* danger today in joining the official church?" Mee Lei asked her.

The lady's face clouded. "I know there is a group there who pretend to be Christians, but who are really placed in the church by the communists themselves. When I was younger and attended university, this same group pretended to be friendly. I thought they were Christians and shared openly with them. When they learned all about my activities, they reported me to the authorities, and I was expelled from the place."

"Why then do you think the church was opened?" Mee Lei asked her.

"To impress the tourists," she replied. "It's really a government-run thing, you know. The Three-Self pastor is hired by the government, and they pay him a good wage for being there.

"You know, it is no longer wise to offer Bibles to the officials in that church. They have a new policy now. Before, they used to say they did not need any. But now they are more clever. Now they will say "yes," and when you bring them Bibles, they will accept them, and either destroy them, or put them in some place where it is hard for Christians to get to them." The woman's words didn't surprise us.*

*This account was typical of that of thousands, probably millions. In fact, prior to publication, a new wave of short-

Brother Andrew had also explained why some believers might shrink from public worship. "When Christians in the suffering church get an official Bible, they often place themselves at great risk. Having to register their names with the authorities, they become easy targets if the government ever decides to clamp down on religion."

Some Chinese Christians had, in fact, told us that a believer has to register not only his own name, but also the name of the person responsible for leading him to Christ. We could just begin to guess at the government's unstated motives for such a requirement!

The government may be proclaiming its new religious policy with a smile on its face, but the smile may be closer to the satisfied grin on the face of the proverbial tiger. Behind it, no doubt, the teeth are still as sharp as ever.

As far as our active involvement was concerned, Project Rainbow had come to an end. On the day we were scheduled to leave China, Eugene got a surprise farewell visit from Chang Lo, the guide he had led to the Lord earlier that year.

One of Chang Lo's co-workers who had once met us told him we were at the hotel. It was Chang Lo's last day in that particular city and our last day in China.

Eugene asked him if he needed any money, but Chang Lo said that money would only create a problem for him.

"You have given me the Lord. That is enough. God bless you! You are my spiritual father."

term imprisonment and interrogation of house-church leaders was begun. Believers inside are deeply burdened that more might follow.

NINETEEN
CHINA'S NUMBER ONE ENEMY

If Eugene was Chang Lo's spiritual father, then certainly Mrs. Kwang was spiritual mother to many thousands in China. During our many long hours of preparation for Project Rainbow, Daniel had finished recounting the moving story of his family's life behind the Bamboo Curtain.

"My mother was eighteen years old when she began to preach in our little church. The Lord had given her several gifts and the church started growing very fast. But the government had started closing down churches and after one year they came to her area.

"She did not know it then, but the authorities had planned to arrest her and her co-workers on a certain night. In prayer that morning she was warned by the Lord to leave town. That night, the officers arrived and nailed the doors of our church. Then they went to the homes of many of the believers and co-workers and hauled them into prison trucks."

"How did they know where to find these people?" I asked.

"Oh, they got their names from the church register which had been introduced under the Three-Self movement.

"Anyway, once in prison, they were treated very badly. Thousands and thousands were killed. Others were tortured and offered freedom if they denied Christ and informed on the other Christians. Many are still in prison.

"When my mother returned, she realized what had happened and cried very, very much. She wanted to be with the believers even if it meant going to prison. But soon the Lord again warned her to leave the area."

The Kwang family had suffered particularly over the fact that their own grandfather was among those taken to jail. The prison guards had been instructed to make a point of using violence on the prisoners. One very sadistic guard armed with a bottle had entered the old man's cell.

"Here, Grandfather, I have a present for you," he said, bringing it down on the old man's head with a crash.

The blow was so savage that it broke a blood vessel in his skull. The internal bleeding lasted for days, and eventually the authorities had to admit him to a nearby hospital. After a few weeks, his pain-wracked body could fight no longer. Grandfather Kwang went to be with the Lord.

Mrs. Kwang knew that she couldn't preach openly, so she took a job as a school teacher. Still she prayed and wept before the Lord, telling Him she wanted to preach again. In 1958 the Lord told her, "I want you to stand up and preach the gospel. You are to be a boat of refuge in the turbulent sea of China. And I will stand beside you."

The next day, her former co-workers who were not in prison started coming to her with the explanation that the Lord had spoken to them about standing up and preaching the gospel. "Now is the time," He had told them.

After two days, the group met for prayer and discussion. God soon began leading them to individuals and families who were ready to hear His Word.

"One time when my mother was in prayer," Daniel said, "the Lord told her to go to a particular street and visit an old lady on the point of death. 'Preach the gospel to her and pray for her,' the Lord directed her.

"My mother did as the Lord told her. She found an old lady in pain with a swollen stomach. As my mother shared the gospel with her, the woman began weeping and accepted the Lord. Then as my mother began to pray for the woman, she was immediately healed.

"Her family could hardly believe it. They were amazed to see their desperately ill grandmother well again. My mother then explained the way of the Lord to the rest of the household. And each one accepted Jesus Christ that same day.

"The one we call 'Old Man' was also clearly led in his ministry. As he asked God to show him where he should preach, he was told to visit a nearby town and witness to a certain man there. The Old Man cried out, 'Lord, I have never been to this place. How can I possibly do what you're asking?' But the Lord said, 'You go, and I will lead you.'

"So the Old Man went and found the town. When he got there, the Lord took him to the street and the home. As he stood outside the house, he prayed again, 'Lord, I don't know this man. I don't even know his name!' But then through prayer, God gave him the name, which he shouted for the person inside to hear.

"When the man inside heard his name being called, he opened the door. The Old Man entered and said, 'Today the salvation of the Lord is come to your home!' Then he explained how the Lord had led him to the house. He began to preach the gospel to the entire family, and they all accepted Jesus Christ and became believers."

At this point in Daniel's story, Mrs. Kwang spoke, as her son translated. "Brother David, my mother wants you to know that there were many,

many more examples like these. There was nothing unusual in the leading she and the Old Man received. All the co-workers were led this way."

As she and her co-workers preached in groups of two at one time, many signs of God's power and love were demonstrated. People saw God's power through miracles, and many were led to Christ. "Your God is both true and living," they would declare.

Mrs. Kwang added more of her own comment. "When these signs and miracles occurred, we always took them as an opportunity to tell people about the greatness of our God. We explained that this same Jesus called upon them to be born again of the Spirit, as it says in John 3. So the Lord used His miracles to win many more people to Himself."

Daniel picked up the story. He told us that his father had taught school while his mother was out preaching. Mr. Kwang's pay had been cut back since the authorities knew about his commitment to Christ. He had to support six people but was earning less than twenty dollars a month.

Whenever a co-worker needed rice, vegetables, or even a ticket to travel for the Lord, they would give whatever they had. Often after Mr. Kwang's pay day, they would be out of money again.

Daniel said, "We didn't have enough food to eat. One bowl of rice would be divided among the six of us twice a day. Frequently, it was cooked in a great deal of water so our bowls could be filled to the brim, mostly with water and just a little rice. This went on so long that my brother and I often found our hands, feet, and bodies swollen from the lack of food.

"Many times my brother and I went out looking for vegetables. We went to the markets and brought home any old ones which the sellers had thrown away. One time we must have eaten something very bad. We got a very serious case of food poisoning, and both of us came close to death.

"Sometimes we just ate the peelings from vegetables, the bark of trees, and sometimes nuts and berries if we could find them. One time my brother was so sick from hunger that he picked up chicken dung and ate it!

"Our life was very hard." He looked at his parents with a smile. "Yet somehow it did not seem hard to us, because at that time our mother and father were not in prison.

"Even after the start of the Cultural Revolution, mother continued preaching from city to city. Because all church buildings in China were closed, services had to be held in private homes.

"Every morning my mother prayed from 3:00 A.M. until 6:30 A.M., unburdening her heart to the Lord and praising Him for all that He was doing. We could see the Lord's power very clearly."

It was not unusual for a group of co-workers to pray all night, waiting on the Lord for His message to the people for the following day. When their sermons were preached, it was common for hundreds to be won to the Lord.

As the church grew, however, so did the attention of the authorities. They had one particularly powerful weapon by which to control the local people. If persecution of parents failed in winning them to the communist line of thought, the authorities often turned to the children.

"One afternoon," Daniel told us, "my older brother Peter was walking through a park on his way to our home. Suddenly a group of people confronted him and beat him up. When he got home he was very sick; he had many wounds and had been hurt very badly.

"A few evenings later, the Red Guards came to our home and took all we had—furniture, clothes, everything. The house was empty when they finished!

"The guards made us all stand up on a bench and told us to deny Jesus Christ. When we would not, they became very angry and beat all of us, even my three-year-old sister, with clubs. After that, they took us to a public square and made a big crowd gather around us.

"The men took my parents and whipped them. They tied them at a forty-five degree angle with a heavy rope and beat their backs with shoes that had sharp spikes in them. 'All right, Kwang, you're going to a labor camp, and let's see how long you hold out there,' a senior official told my father.

"'Even if I die, I will not deny Jesus Christ,' he said. Then they hauled him off to a terrible camp where people were dying daily from ill treatment."

Peter, Daniel's older brother, watched the sorrow in his mother's face as her husband was taken away. He was also aware of something strange within his own body. When they returned home, he knew it was serious. A number of veins had ruptured, and he had begun to hemorrhage. The boy's earlier assault, on top of the beating and shock he received that day, had proved too much for his body to bear.

Not wanting to worry her further, Peter quietly retreated to a dark corner of the house. He used a few soiled rags left by the soldiers and mopped up the blood seeping from his body.

After several hours he knew his condition was too serious to keep from his mother any longer and called for her help.

Close to despair after seeing the bleeding, Mrs. Kwang prayed for the bleeding to stop—and it did. Then she washed and lovingly laid him on the floor for the night.

In another room, she fell on her knees and prayed, "Father, you know I can't stand any more. I've already had my husband taken from me. Please don't allow my son to die. It would break me." Then, after some struggle, she added, "If it is your will, Lord. I'll be obedient."

Sobbing in prayer, she sensed the presence of the Lord beside her, comforting her. His voice came in reply, "Your son has undergone too much persecution already. Now it is time to take him home. He has suffered enough. He is pure."

Within a few weeks, twelve-year-old Peter Kwang was dead.

Many years later, just before Mrs. Kwang was to leave China, she heard from a pastor who had been working in the Three-Self church movement. The man explained that he had been the instigator of the attack on young Peter in the park. He begged her forgiveness.

The Lord did not allow Mrs. Kwang to be crushed by the death of her son. As she reached out to Him, He comforted her. In time she was on her feet, once more faithfully testifying for the Lord. She and her dedicated team traveled days at a time, proclaiming the gospel from town to town.

One time after a woman was healed, Mrs. Kwang taught the new believers songs for worship. The local cadres heard children singing them in the street and thus became aware of her ministry in their town. Outraged, they began an intensive search for Christians. Those caught were thrown into prison and beaten until finally one of them cracked and informed on the rest.

"Find that woman and arrest her," the authorities said. So, one day while she was at home with her children, they arrested her and took her to trial before a tribunal of communist officials. Her wrists were tightly bound, and she was forced to bend down from the waist at a ninety-degree angle as they questioned her. If she gave an answer they didn't like, a guard would kick or hit her viciously on the back.

Every six hours the guards changed shift, and a fresh group came in to question and torture her. During the three-day period, she was allowed no water, food, or sleep.

Yet though bent double in agony, all Mrs. Kwang could speak of was the love of Jesus.

"I have seen God with my own eyes," she told her persecutors and proceeded to tell them of a period, some years earlier, when she had contracted five very serious illnesses at one time. Her weight had halved, and she had become desperately sick, with no hope of recovery.

"Finally I knew I was on the point of death itself. I could breathe only with little short gasps, and I felt certain I would be dead within a few minutes.

"But just then, the Lord came to me and comforted me. He showed me a vision of the Second Coming when He will return to this earth to take His children home. And, at the same time, He healed me completely.

"So you see," she concluded with a smile, "now I must preach the gospel. I must tell people of the greatness of our God. And let them know that He loves them and wants them to live forever with Him.

"He loves you too," she added. "You can find new life in Him. Are you willing to believe?"

As Mrs. Kwang finished her story, the officials were furious. But they couldn't deny that through her attitude, they were seeing God's forgiveness and love. Slowly a few responded; some began to weep. Soon one said that he too wanted a faith like hers. Others then followed until many in the interrogation room accepted Christ.

"After the three days," Daniel said, "my mother was thrown into a cell. It was terrible. The tiny room was underground, so my mother was in darkness. The toilet had not been cleaned in a long time. There was no bed for her to sleep on, only the damp floor. When they threw her in there, she finally lost consciousness.

"But the Lord is faithful." A slight smile lit up his face. "He came to her in a dream and comforted her. Then He told her to go on preaching for Him, even in that shocking place.

"My mother drew on His strength alone. She told Him she would obey, but she could not see how she could witness. It seemed impossible. Then the Lord showed her a way. She went to the prison authorities with a suggestion. 'I can see that this prison is very dirty,' she said. 'Would you like me to do some hard labor for you and clean it?'

"The authorities were very responsive to the idea. Soon every part of the prison was open to her. She could preach to all the prisoners and was warmly welcomed. They were touched by her love for them. Through it they saw the love of God Himself, and hundreds gave their lives to the Lord as a result. The guards were also touched by my mother's attitude to them and to the authorities. Instead of hatred and bitterness, they were meeting one whose Lord had said, 'Love your enemies. Do good to them that hate you.' As she taught them about the Lord, many guards became Christians as well.

"But," Daniel continued, with a shake of his head, "when the communist authorities heard about it, they were furious and beat her all over again. It was bad, very bad. Then a high officer sent my mother some blank paper and told her to write out her confession. She prayed for guidance and began to write out the biblical plan of salvation. When she sent it to the official, he was furious with her because he had to read it before a large group of officers who would judge her. When they heard my mother's statement, many of them became Christians too!"

Nevertheless, Mrs. Kwang was sentenced to twenty years in prison and was interrogated again. They tied her according to the "super-binding" method, one of their most effective means of getting information from prisoners. A rope is tied from the base of the neck down to the hands which are bound behind the back. It is impossible to get one's hands comfortable without giving the neck a rope burn. To make the neck comfortable means breaking the wrists.

This excruciating torture lasted for several days. Then, during morning prayer, the Lord told her that she would be released that same day. Despite her twenty-year sentence, she believed and waited expectantly for the promise to be fulfilled. By evening, however, she had heard nothing.

She knew the prison allowed no release of inmates after nightfall. But her confidence in the Lord was unshaken. Then at nine o'clock, an official came to her cell.

"Okay, you! You can leave the prison now," he shouted. "Don't you tell anybody about the torture and the beatings. Don't mention these things. If you do, it will mean trouble for you. Now, get out of here! Get home!"

The next day Mrs. Kwang began to preach again. She didn't know why the prison rule had been broken. "It was the Lord," she told us. In the same way, the Lord blessed her ministry in the months which followed. Hundreds of new believers joined fellowship groups and training classes. Among them were former Red Guards and prison officers who now addressed her as "Mama Kwang."

"There are presently 300 such fellowship groups in my area," Daniel told us. "The small ones have just a few hundred—the big ones, several thousand."

"You mean all together, surely?" I asked him. The area he was referring to was one-third the size of California. The numbers seemed impossible.

"No. In *each* group there is that number," Daniel repeated patiently. Then, as he read the surprise on our faces, he added, with a cheerful smile, "It is the Lord's doing! He is very wonderful to us."

Eventually the secret police caught up with Mrs. Kwang again. She was imprisoned two more times. On her last time, the evangelist was sentenced for life. Because of the seriousness of her "crime," her husband was led from his labor camp to her prison.

"Your wife has committed many crimes against the State," the prison guard told him. "We consider her a maximum security prisoner. It would be too great a risk to let her loose in the community ever again." With hatred blazing in his eyes, the official said, "We regard your wife as China's number one enemy!"

Mr. Kwang then tried to visit her inside the prison, but was forbidden. Wanting to comfort his wife somehow, he slowly began walking around the outside of the prison. Along the walk, he sang hymns his wife knew well. He hoped that wherever she was in the building, she would hear the hymns and be strengthened.

Before his return to the labor camp, Mr. Kwang said goodbye to his children. His parting words were, "If you can get to see your mother, tell her that I am of the same heart as she is. Tell her I love her. Explain that because I was not permitted to see her in prison, I walked around it and sang songs of the Lord. I wanted to comfort her. Tell your mother these things."

TWENTY
RUNNING TOGETHER

"What's next, Daddy?" Dawn asked amid the noise of our favorite Chinese restaurant in Manila. "Where will you go from here?"

I knew the answer. We had already heard reports of Christians traveling two or three days to get one of the 30,000 Project Rainbow Bibles. The next step could only be the million which the Kwangs had requested the day they arrived from China.

"Can we trust the Lord for a million?" I grinned, watching their surprised reaction. Then the other three nodded with understanding.

"I guess it fits the vision the Lord gave you, doesn't it?" Julie said.

"You bet! After all, He said at the start it should be ten million. This is only one-tenth of that amount. Not so much after all, is it?" I chuckled.

"Think of the people, Bibles, money, and prayer support you'll need, Dad," said David. "Blows my mind!"

"Mine, too!" I replied. "And yet, so did each of the other steps we've taken. First the deliveries of the 40s, and the 50s, then the 900, and finally, the 30,000. Compared to the size of the step before, each one seemed big at the time."

"Yet the Lord was bigger still," Julie murmured.

"And He can do it again this time," I smiled. After all, He's the same Lord!"

On my next trip to Hong Kong, I discussed the

task with the Kwang family. This time one of our Chinese staff translated.

"Yes," Mr. Kwang said with a smile, "I believe it is the next step, Brother David. But it will not happen without the Lord. It will take a giant of a miracle to move one million Scriptures inside China."

"It'll take several miracles," I replied. "One to get that number of Bibles supplied, one to move them all past communist barriers, and another to find people willing to distribute them inside. But I'm prepared to trust the Lord with you."

Mrs. Kwang commented, "You remember when Joshua called on the Lord to stop the sun and the moon so they could win the battle? It will take a mighty work of God for us to be victorious in this battle too. But God has already shown He can do the impossible."

She smiled warmly and paused a moment before continuing. "And the hunger of the believers is so great, Brother David, so great. Even with Project Rainbow, your Bibles are not enough."

Together we read some of the many letters which had begun pouring into our offices from the heart of China. They were written in the special language of the suffering church:

Dear Cousin:
Just as we were filled with yearning . . . we were satisfied. Our hunger was not because we had no bread, nor our thirst because we lacked water. Rather it was because we did not have the precious Word which God has given us. . . . Thus, when we received it, it was just like being in a desert and seeing an oasis. Our hearts are filled with inexpressible happiness. . . .

We read another like it.

Beloved Cousin:

What we had lost earlier . . . you have replaced: The Bread of Life. . . .

After receiving the Bread of Life, we brothers and sisters here have been offering up praise and thanksgiving. At the same time, we have been devouring the Bread of Life. . . . It gives us strength, enabling us to walk the path laid down ahead of us, to fight the good fight. We will not disappoint your concern for us. . . .

As I looked over the letters, I wondered how many other thousands and even millions of believers in China needed that same hunger satisfied.

"I have a name for this project: *Project Pearl*," I told the Kwangs.

Their faces lit up. "The pearl of great price?" they asked.

"That's right. The one precious pearl for which the merchant gave all that he had."

"Just like the believers in China," mused Mrs. Kwang. "They, too, have given all they have to belong to the Kingdom of God."

"Everything," I said. "And that's why we want to stand behind them." *Why can't we in the West give at least some, if not all, of what we have for that same Kingdom?* I thought.

We had heard the first-hand accounts of God's abundant blessing from the Kwang family. Even in the face of severe persecution, they had trusted the Lord. I recalled the vision Mrs. Kwang told me about in Hong Kong.

"I saw many thousands of co-workers in both the East and the West, working side by side and digging a trench. That trench became bigger and longer, and then water started to flow into it.

"This water was the River of Life. I saw it flow first through China into all parts of the country,

215

and after that into the whole world."

Daniel's father had added his own word of explanation.

"The Lord gave her this vision in 1974, in that dreadful prison where it was hardest for her to believe. She had been sentenced to life in an underground cell with no toilet facilities except a bucket in the corner which was never emptied. The cell was damp and crawling with lice and mosquitoes. Rice cooked with sand was her only food. And she had already been beaten and tortured terribly and was still being interrogated by the authorities.

"At that time it seemed she could not survive very long in such a place. Yet when the Lord gave her that vision, she believed Him. And after He miraculously released her from prison, she told us all that He had shown her."

Mrs. Kwang finished the story herself. "It was the time, Brother David, when you were just beginning your ministry in the Free World for those under persecution for their faith. It was as the Lord told me. I did not know it then, but East and West were already working together to dig the channel for the River of Life to flow."

There had been many occasions when I had wondered whether I was crazy to contemplate a ministry to China, particularly in 1974. Mrs. Kwang's vision was added confirmation of the Lord's authorizing the ministry!

At that point in our conversation, all of us bowed silently before the One who had brought both vision and ministry together.

Then, Daniel said, "Oh, there is one other story I would like to tell you, Brother David. I have witnessed the goodness of the Lord with my own eyes. It happened a long time ago when my mother was first imprisoned and my father was in labor camp. She had been taken away after my brother

Peter died—just a short while after our house had been emptied of all its furniture, money, and food. We had to sleep on the floor.

"When the guards had taken my mother, they'd instructed the neighbors to torture and beat us children so that we would deny our faith in the Lord. We didn't. But my heart was very heavy. I was ten years old with a younger brother and sister to look after.

"At that time we had only a little bit of rice in a jar. With no money we could not buy any more. And nobody could come to help us because the secret police were standing guard nearby to prevent them.

"We realized that if we cooked the rice that day, there would be none left for the next. Then we would just have to wait for death to come. The three of us threw ourselves down upon the floor and asked the Lord to perform a powerful miracle. Then in faith we began to cook the rice.

"Next day when we woke up for our breakfast, we went to the rice jar. The Lord had answered our prayer. There was just as much rice as there had been the day before.

"And every day it was the same. The Lord did not allow the level of rice to go down. We had enough until the day my mother was released from prison and then it ran dry."

A smile gently broke over his porcelain-like features. "The Lord is very wonderful in my life," he said.

Sitting beside Daniel, I looked at him and his family with tears in my eyes. It wasn't the first time my heart felt ready to burst and words escaped me. They and their brethren inside China were a living testimony to the greatness of God.

In that moment I had learned an unforgettable lesson. I had originally come to work, thinking of the ministry we would be able to give the suffering church. But now the truth of the situation hit me. How much greater was *their* ministry to *us*—the free church in the West full of opportunities to learn of God and yet negligent about discovering how He really works.

"Daniel," I asked, "how is it that your brethren walk so close to the Lord? I don't know of many in the West who hear the Lord's voice in the way you do."

It was true. These people trusted the Lord so much that they were prepared to follow Him through the most horrendous circumstances with childlike trust and simplicity. They obeyed unquestioningly. Did one have to *suffer* before reaching that kind of spiritual walk?

Daniel passed my question on to his parents. "One has to make the sacrifice, Brother David, to follow the Lord this way."

"You mean that one has to be persecuted before having this kind of faith?" I asked.

"No, that is not the sacrifice. The sacrifice they are talking about is *prayer*."

I looked at them and tried to grasp their meaning. Then it came. These believers, and the thousands of others in China, didn't give the Lord just a few minutes of their day in prayer. Their *entire* day was like one extended prayer.

They were so hungry for the Lord that at any given opportunity they would seek His presence. Often praying for hours at a time, they poured out their hearts, offering themselves for His service.

"Daniel, would you ask your parents how long it takes to reach that kind of commitment—to be so given over to Jesus? How many hours of prayer each day? How many weeks, months, years?"

The gentle answer came back: "The Lord knows your heart, David."

There it was. If the heart were "sacrificed" to Him, if the believer so abandoned himself to the

218

Lord that nothing else mattered, then the rest would follow.

This, then, was the pathway to such a walk with God.

A few weeks after discussing Project Pearl with the Kwangs, I went with Shan and Roger Winthrop, one of his colleagues, to visit Wang MingDao, a man well known inside China and through out the Christian world. Along with Watchman Nee, he had been a major leader of the Chinese Church until his imprisonment in 1955.

After fourteen months of prison life, however, Wang MingDao finally signed a confession admitting that his opposition to the Three-Self movement had been "counter-revolutionary." He was released, but became severely disturbed emotionally. Recognizing he'd been brainwashed, he rejected his confession and was again sent to prison where he stayed for twenty-one years and eight months. In January 1980, he was released to join his wife who had been freed two years earlier.

We expected to see a quiet, aged man, perhaps broken in body and in spirit. Instead, as with Mrs. Kwang, we found a believer with the same fire for the Lord we had heard about in his younger days.

"I remember the words of Jesus to His Church in Revelation 2:10:

Fear none of those things which thou shalt suffer: behold, the devil shall cast some of you into prison, that ye may be tried; and ye shall have tribulation ten days: be thou faithful unto death, and I will give thee a crown of life.

These verses strengthened me while I was in prison.

"I have been through twenty-three years of refining, and the Lord has not allowed me to suffer loss through it all, but rather to receive an even greater blessing.

"Twenty-five years ago, I'd forgotten that Satan was waiting to use my weakest point to attack me. 'Aren't you afraid?' he asked. And he brought me face to face with a terror that I had never experienced before. Never in my life had I confronted anything so fearsome, and I, like Peter, was weak.

"Well, what happened in the end? After the Lord Jesus rose from the dead, he appeared first of all to this fallen Peter. Now my Lord has done the same with me. He has not remonstrated against me, but instead has comforted me. The Bible says, 'A bruised reed he shall not break, a smoking flax he shall not quench.'"

The old man had the light of battle in his eyes as he talked about the dangers of fear. He related a folk tale to illustrate his point.

"In my book, *An Anthology of Spiritual Food*, I quoted a Middle Eastern tale:

One day, a mayor of Baghdad left the city and journeyed outside. On the road he met a fearful creature, a Djinn. He asked the Djinn, "Where are you going?"

The Djinn replied "I'm off to Baghdad and this time, I'm going to take the lives of a thousand people."

The mayor was very dismayed. "Oh, this time we're going to lose a thousand souls to the evil Djinn." But when he returned to the city, he saw that the dead numbered several times more than what the Djinn had said. He said, "The Djinn has deceived me! The number of the dead far exceed that which the Djinn told me. If I meet him again, I'll ask him why he should say such things."

Some time later, he met the Djinn on the road again and said, "Djinn, you lied to me! The people who died in Baghdad were many more than you said!"

The Djinn replied, "The people I killed were exactly according to the number I told you. The rest were those who died of fright!"

"So I used that little story and entitled it: 'Still More Die From Fright.'

At that point, Roger leaned toward Shan. "I wonder how we would have reacted in America?" he whispered softly. "Or any of us in the West? Would we have given over to fear? Or could we have held firm for twenty-three years of prison?"

The old teacher continued. "Now there is only One I fear: God. So long as I do not sin against God and remain faithful to Him, I fear nothing. Each day that we spend on earth we must be on our guard.

"There is an ancient Chinese saying: 'There are many beginnings but few endings.' The Bible records many stories of people who began and never finished. And I must warn myself: never be one who begins and cannot finish."

"His message couldn't have been more appropriate, could it?" said an exuberant Brother Andrew as I recounted my unforgettable meeting with Wang MingDao. Accompanied by James Wee, I was in Holland for our yearly international meeting. The three of us were walking through the cobbled streets of Brother Andrew's picturesque hometown.

James spoke up. "And we have no time to lose! Some believers in China have already told us to get Bibles inside as quickly as possible. They are convinced God is warning them that China will not remain so open for long. I've heard the same thing from believers throughout the country.

"In fact, the door of China has never been so

open. And on the other side of it, there are now one billion people who need to know Jesus Christ— one-fourth of the world's population!"

With Zhao Ziyang in power, the country would be more open than ever in the immediate future.

"That's what makes Project Pearl so important," Brother Andrew said. "I believe you have to make it priority number one. And be assured that the rest of us will be standing behind you."

The three of us walked down the road leading to the nearby harbor. As we sat on a wooden bench near the water's edge, I pulled my Bible from my briefcase. In it was a letter from China.

"I'd like you to hear this, Brother Andrew. I've heard the translation already. And it's really something."

The letter had been written by the "Old Man" who had been such a support to the Kwang family's ministry. James Wee translated it:

Beloved Cousin David, safety and peace!

We thank God for His great mercy in lending you to us to care for us. The precious books you sent were received today. . . . Thank you for your love and concern. If you have opportunity, we are honoring and inviting you to visit our town. Then we can have fellowship together, share the grace of the Lord, and encourage each other to run for the Lord until He returns. . . ."

"'Encourage each other to run for the Lord,'" Brother Andrew repeated. "Not just the two of you, David, but the body of believers inside China, and the church in the Free World, encouraging each other to run for the Lord.

"Why not?" he continued. "If one million, or ultimately ten million, Bibles are to go into the People's Republic, they could do with at least that number of Christians behind them. That would mean one person praying for each Bible and for the believer who receives it."

I watched a pair of fishermen in a small boat approaching the shore. A young boy was at the tiller. As they reached the shallow waters, his father leaped out, holding a thick rope. Father and son worked as one: The boy steered, while his father waded through the flotsam to guide the boat to the bank.

"Amen," I said. "East and West need to work together! The suffering church needs our prayer support and our provision of the Word. And we, in the Free World, need their witness and challenge, as well as their unfailing prayer support."

"You know what it reminds me of?" James said with a smile. "Another letter you got from China—the very first one the Kwangs ever sent to you personally."

"Yes," I said, recalling it clearly. "One sentence in it was my favorite. It was the one Mrs. Kwang wrote: 'So, then, let us run *together*!'"

For further information on Open Doors' ministry to the suffering church, please write:

Open Doors with Brother Andrew
International Headquarters
P.O. Box 47
3840AA Harderwijk, Holland

Open Doors with Brother Andrew
P.O. Box 2020
Orange, California 92669

Open Doors with Brother Andrew
P.O. Box 4282
Manila, Philippines

Open Doors with Brother Andrew
Box 61
Station D
Toronto M6P 3J5
Canada